CULTURE SMART!
NETHERLANDS

Sheryl Buckland

914.92
BUC
2016

·K·U·P·E·R·A·R·D·

ISBN 978 1 85733 881 2
British Library Cataloguing in Publication Data
A CIP catalogue entry for this book is available from the British Library

First published in Great Britain
by Kuperard, an imprint of Bravo Ltd
59 Hutton Grove, London N12 8DS
Tel: +44 (0) 20 8446 2440 Fax: +44 (0) 20 8446 2441
www.culturesmart.co.uk
Inquiries: sales@kuperard.co.uk

Series Editor Geoffrey Chesler
Design Bobby Birchall

Printed in India

About the Author

SHERYL BUCKLAND is an English management trainer and business studies tutor who lived for sixteen years in the Netherlands, and who has worked for public and private organizations in both Britain and the Netherlands. A member of the British Chartered Institute of Personnel Development, she holds an M.A. in Education and an M.A. in Social Sciences. While living in the Netherlands, Sheryl immersed herself in Dutch culture, conducting research on cultural acclimatization, the role of Dutch-language teachers, and child development. During this time she also worked as an Associate Lecturer for the British Open University Business School, and as a Business Communications Tutor for undergraduates in the Utrecht Hogeschool's Faculty of Economics and Management. She and her husband now live in Stratford-upon-Avon, but she retains close links with the Netherlands through her Dutch and expatriate friends and regular visits.

The Culture Smart! series is continuing to expand. All Culture Smart! guides are available as e-books, and many as audio books. For latest titles visit

www.culturesmart.co.uk

The publishers would like to thank **CultureSmart!**Consulting for its help in researching and developing the concept for this series.

CultureSmart!Consulting creates tailor-made seminars and consultancy programs to meet a wide range of corporate, public-sector, and individual needs. Whether delivering courses on multicultural team building in the USA, preparing Chinese engineers for a posting in Europe, training call-center staff in India, or raising the awareness of police forces to the needs of diverse ethnic communities, it provides essential, practical, and powerful skills worldwide to an increasingly international workforce.

For details, visit www.culturesmartconsulting.com

CultureSmart!Consulting and **CultureSmart!** guides have both contributed to and featured regularly in the weekly travel program "Fast Track" on BBC World TV.

contents

contents

Map of the Netherlands

introduction

Culture Smart! Netherlands is written for those travelers who want to get to the heart of the country. It describes the main features of Dutch society and culture and offers insights and practical advice on what to expect and how to behave in different circumstances.

In painting this picture it has been necessary to use a broad brush. Generalizations, of course, have their limitations. For every description of a "typical Dutch person in a typical situation" there will be somebody who behaves quite differently. However, over the centuries certain national characteristics have evolved. The Dutch are renowned for their organizational skills and their commercial acumen. They are known for being hospitable, friendly, pragmatic, tolerant, fair-minded, and just. They are famous for their struggle to control the sea that constantly threatens to flood their land, and their hydraulic engineers are highly regarded throughout the world. At the height of its power in the seventeenth century, this small seafaring nation led Europe and the world in cultural and scientific endeavor, and laid the foundations for the modern age.

This book covers different aspects of Dutch life. The chapters on social values and attitudes and on the way business is conducted offer psychological insights and practical advice that will help in your personal and professional dealings with Dutch people. Personal vignettes and case studies illustrate the general points. Other sections provide background information on geography, politics, and government. One of the most important of these is the brief historical outline—a people are their collective memory, and Dutch history and contemporary culture are closely intertwined.

There is also more general information—for instance on travel, accommodation, and festivals in the Netherlands. You can use the index or the extended contents pages to dip into sections that particularly interest you, or you can start at the beginning and work through from cover to cover.

Culture Smart! Netherlands introduces you to the inner life of the Dutch people and the subtle complexities of their culture. As the historian Simon Schama says in *The Embarrassment of Riches*: "But if there is one Dutch culture, there are many rooms within it . . . it can swim with variety yet remain coherent unto itself. And such puzzles divert. They can even instruct."

Great riches await the visitor. Enjoy your reading!

culture smart! netherlands

Key Facts

Offical Name	The Kingdom of the Netherlands	(Koninkrijk der Nederlanden)
Capital City	Amsterdam	
Main Cities	The Hague, Rotterdam, Utrecht, Maastricht	
Area	16,033 square miles (41,526 sq. km).	Approx. the size of Massachusetts and Connecticut combined
Climate	Temperate	
Currency	Euro. Since January 1, 2002	
Population	17.1 million	
Ethnic Makeup	78% Dutch, 2 2% other	About 12% are of non-Western European origin: Turkish, Moroccan, Surinamese, Antillean.
Language	Dutch and Frisian (only spoken in Friesland)	In the Dutch Antilles English and Papiamento are also spoken.
Religion	44% unaffiliated, 29% Roman Catholic, 19% Protestant, and 8% other, including 6% Muslim, 1% Hindu, and 1% Buddhist	
Government	The Netherlands is a constitutional monarchy. The monarch is head of state – currently King Willem-Alexander. The prime minister is the head of government. There are 12 provinces.	
Dependent Areas	Aruba and the Dutch Antilles	

Media	The Dutch Broadcasting Association (De Nederlandse Omroep Stichting) coordinates broadcasting on the national television and radio networks. There are public and commercial channels on both TV and radio.	There are very many national and regional newspapers and magazines.
Media: English Language	English-language daily newspapers (American and British) can be bought at main railway stations and from some newsdealers and book shops. Several Dutch English-language publications cater to expatriates and businesspeople. See www.expatica.com/nl or www.dutchnews.nl for a daily summary of the Dutch news.	
Electricity	220 volts, 50 Hz	
DVD Players	American DVDs are incompatible with Dutch systems.	
Telephone	The country code for the Netherlands is 31.	To dial out, dial 00. Private companies may have special codes.
Internet Domain	.nl	
Time Zone	The Netherlands is in the Central European Time Zone (CET), which is UTC/GMT + 1 hr. Normally EST + 6hrs	Daylight saving in summer is UTC/GMT + 2 hrs.

chapter one

LAND & PEOPLE

The Netherlands is often referred to as Holland, which is actually the name of two of its twelve provinces. This small country on the northwestern seaboard of Europe occupies an area of 16,033 square miles (41,526 sq. km) and is densely populated. The majority of the 17.1 million people who live there are concentrated in the west, especially within the Randstad—"Rim Town," or urban conglomeration— the irregularly shaped area lying between Amsterdam, The Hague, Rotterdam, and Utrecht. The areas of thinnest population are in the north of the country.

The Dutch have spent centuries battling against the sea, to keep it from flowing into and over low-lying parts of the land. This constant fight against the elements is said to have been a key influence in forming their general character, as well as particular aspects of Dutch society. While the water has been an enemy in some respects, it has been harnessed as an ally in others. A maritime nation, the Dutch set to sea early in their history to trade with other countries. The network of rivers and canals within the country has been used for transportation and as part of their defenses, and more recently for leisure activities.

The Netherlands has a mixed reputation abroad. Some believe it to be a country where "anything goes" because of its liberal attitude toward soft drugs, prostitution, homosexuality, and matters such as euthanasia. While it is true that many Dutch laws are very liberal, this gives only a partial picture of attitudes in the country as a whole. Other people abroad focus on the Dutch reputation for tolerance, concern for justice, and respect for human rights. This, too, is an important element of Dutch culture, but again it belies the complexities of life in the Netherlands today.

GEOGRAPHICAL OVERVIEW

The Netherlands is bounded to the north and west by the North Sea, to the east by Germany, and to the south by Belgium. It is about the size of Massachusetts and Connecticut together, or the area of the south of England. Situated at the mouths of three major European rivers, the Rhine, the Meuse or Maas, and the Scheldt, its name Nederland ("low land") refers

to its low-lying nature. Holland, similarly, means "land in a hollow." Just over a quarter of the country is below sea level, and much of the rest is at or just above it, which makes flooding along its 280-mile (425-km) coastline the greatest natural hazard. The lowest point is at Zuidplaspolder—22 feet (6.7 m) below sea level. There is a constant battle to keep nature under control and the sea at bay. Because of this the Dutch have excelled at hydraulic engineering. Dikes are used extensively to prevent flooding. The largest of these is the 20-mile (32-km) long Afsluitdijk (the "Closing Dike"), which was constructed in the early 1930s, joining the provinces of North Holland and Friesland via the road that runs along the top of it. The dike closed off the North Sea and turned part of the Zuiderzee into what is now a freshwater lake—the Ijsselmeer. The Afsluitdijk made it possible to drain parts of the Ijsselmeer and turn them into *polders* (land reclaimed from under the water). This reclaimed land now forms the province of Flevoland. The main delta area of the Netherlands forms the southwestern province of Zeeland. It is protected from flooding by an enormous complex of dams and bridges called the Delta Works, built during the 1980s and 1990s, that combine to control the water level.

The landscape of the Netherlands is not totally flat and featureless, as many people expect it to be. There are distinct regional variations: sand dunes and lowland start by the sea in the west and north, leading to the wooded Utrecht *heuvelrug* (hilly ridge) in the center, and the sandy areas in the east of the country. North Brabant and the province of Gelderland contain most of the wooded countryside. There are

also areas of heather-filled heath in Gelderland and in the province of Drenthe. Finally, there are the slightly higher hills in the southeastern province of Limburg, near the borders of Germany and Belgium. The highest point of the Netherlands is in this province, at Vaalserberg Hill, which is 1,053 feet (321 m) above sea level. Each area has its own fauna and flora and there are nature reserves across the country.

To the north of the country are the Wadden Sea Islands (Waddeneilanden). The sea in this area is very shallow, and at low tide at certain times of the year it is possible to take a guided walk across the mudflats from the mainland to the islands at particular points (see page 128).

If you are flying over the Netherlands, the two things that strike you are the amount of water and the regularity of the landscape. The Dutch like things to be neat, and this is evident in the regular patchwork of fields, crisscrossed by waterways. When you are at ground level, the changing quality of the light is impressive. No wonder there have been so many famous Dutch landscape painters.

Windmills were used to harness the energy of the wind in order to pump out water from the lowlands. Many can still be seen, but the vast majority are now simply a charming tourist attraction.

CLIMATE

The climate is temperate. Generally the summers are cool and the winters are mild, but cold snaps can occur in January and February. When the temperatures drop and the canals and lakes freeze over, the Dutch get out their skates and take to the ice. At these times, the skies are a brilliant periwinkle blue, the sun shines, and everybody has a great time in the open air. People take hot-air balloon rides to enjoy the marvelous views.

When you come to the Netherlands, bring an umbrella and waterproof clothes. It can be spring, summer, fall, or winter, but rain is a part of every season. The Dutch make the best of circumstances. At the slightest hint of sunshine, tables and chairs will be out on the café terraces.

A BRIEF HISTORY

In order to understand modern Dutch society, some knowledge of the past is necessary. What follows is a rough sketch of the major periods in the country's history, highlighting some of the individuals who have influenced Dutch thinking.

The Early Years

The earliest inhabitants of the Netherlands were hunter-gatherers who lived on the hills in the center of the country around 150,000 years ago. The last Ice Age drove them away and people did not return until around 9000 BCE. During the Iron Age (from 750 BCE) people began to settle in the lower, more fertile areas. The threat of flooding was very high, so they constructed artificial hills (*terpen*) upon which to build their homes and farms.

The Romans

When Julius Caesar began his conquest of the Netherlands, the northern territories were inhabited by Germanic tribes, who had pushed the earlier Celtic population further south. The Romans controlled the Celtic lands south of the Rhine from 57 BCE to 406 CE, and exerted influence on the Germanic north through trade.

In spite of Roman efforts to control flooding with dams, the sea continually flooded the western part of the Netherlands. Gradually the area turned into a peat bog unfit for people to live in. At the same time, the northern borders were coming under attack. Unrest at the center of the Roman Empire meant that troops were needed closer to home, and in 406 the Romans pulled back, abandoning their forts along the Rhine.

With the departure of the Romans, Germanic culture took hold. The Frisians extended southward, Saxon invaders settled in the east, and Franks overran the area south of the Rhine and the Maas. By the early sixth century the Franks controlled Gaul (present-day France) and northern Italy. The Frankish king, Clovis I, converted to Christianity, and by the eighth century the Franks had imposed Christianity on almost all of the country.

Charlemagne

In 800 Charlemagne, King of the Franks, was crowned Emperor of the Romans by Pope Leo III in Rome. In the Netherlands he installed his counts or princes to administer justice and to organize the collection of taxes. They were also charged with the control of military matters.

In return, they were given land and certain privileges. Gradually the power of these nobles increased. When Charlemagne died in 814 the central authority of the Frankish Empire declined and many of the wealthiest regional nobles ruled practically independently.

From the ninth to the twelfth centuries the Netherlands was repeatedly partitioned in the divisions of the Holy Roman Empire, not falling clearly into either the French or the German kingdoms. From 850 onward, Viking raiders from Scandinavia took advantage of the situation, but Viking raids had ceased entirely by the beginning of the eleventh century.

The Middle Ages

In 925, all of present-day Netherlands was incorporated into the Holy Roman Empire. Larger principalities were formed by consolidating some of the smaller counties. The feudal lords grew stronger and the territories that would later become the Dutch provinces began to be established.

By the fifteenth century a number of towns had become prosperous trading centers. Usually ruled by small groups of merchants, they effectively became self-governing republics. Some joined the Hanseatic League, an organization that protected the trading interests of leading North Sea and Baltic port cities. Citizens within the towns began to exert a strong influence over politics and economic affairs.

In the fifteenth century, all the Low Countries (today's Belgium, Netherlands, and Luxembourg) came under the rule of the dukes of Burgundy. In 1464 some of the regional assemblies tried to resist the centralization imposed upon them by Philip the Good, Duke of Burgundy (1396–1467). They met in Bruges, and the "States-General' (Staten-Generaal), as the assembly was known, thereafter became a part of joint government in the regions.

Religion and Revolt

The discovery of the New World shifted economic power from the Mediterranean to the countries on Europe's western seaboard, and during the sixteenth century the Netherlands grew in importance.

Protestantism found a ready audience among the strong-willed Dutch nobility and merchant class. The Renaissance Humanist scholar Erasmus of Rotterdam (c. 1466–1536) had an enormous influence on the way that educated people throughout Europe thought about the teachings and practices of the Roman Catholic Church. When

the Augustinian monk Martin Luther (1483–1546) challenged the authority of the Church and instigated the Protestant Reformation, there followed a period of bitter religious wars. The exiled French reformer John Calvin (1509–64) established a form of lay theocracy in Geneva that would provide a model for "the most perfect school of Christ."

In 1530, the Habsburg ruler Charles V, King of Spain, was crowned Holy Roman Emperor. In the great political and religious upheaval of the times, he staunchly supported the Pope, and introduced the Inquisition to the Netherlands to deal with heretics. Many Dutch people were tortured and killed.

In 1555, Charles retired to a monastery and handed over the seventeen states of the Netherlands to his son, Philip II (1527–98). Philip chose several

members of the largely Protestant Dutch nobility to act as his governors (*stadhouders*) in the large provinces, but increasingly made decisions without consulting them. His rule of the Netherlands was high-handed, remote, and insensitive to local interests and traditions. He levied heavy taxes and restricted trade in the middle of an economic crisis, and was even more determined to suppress the Protestants than his father.

In spite of, or possibly because of, this, Protestantism took a stronger hold on the people, and the rigid beliefs of Calvinism became even more popular than Lutheranism. Trouble was brewing. When a group of Protestant nobles presented a "Request" for more lenient treatment in 1556, they were described by one Spanish counselor as "beggars," a name they immediately adopted. Soon after this, Calvinist and Anabaptist mobs stormed through Catholic churches in the Netherlands, destroying church treasures and works of art, to the cry of "Long live the Beggars."

William of Nassau, Prince of Orange (1533–84), was the Burgrave of Antwerp and *stadhouder* for Holland, Utrecht, and Zeeland. Increasingly alienated by Spain's policy of centralized rule and religious oppression, in 1567 he refused to renew his allegiance to Philip, and fled the country in the company of many Calvinists to lead the rebellion against Spain. Philip responded by sending an army to the

Netherlands, headed by the ruthlessly effective Duke of Alba. The years that followed saw thousands of rebels killed.

The "Sea Beggars"

William the Silent (as William became known) raised armies in Germany and made several attempts to free territory in the Netherlands from Spanish rule. Defeated on land, he continued the struggle at sea by means of the so-called "Sea Beggars" (*Watergeuzen*). These semi-pirates were Dutch patriots who raided ships carrying merchandise between Spain and the Netherlands, with cautious support from the English. William's aim was to unite the Dutch, Protestant and Catholic, against their common enemy. In 1572 the Sea Beggars captured the port of Brill, from which they established control over the entire Scheldt estuary and the approaches to Antwerp.

The Republic of the North

In 1579 seven northern rebel provinces signed the Union of Utrecht, which is regarded as the foundation charter of the Dutch Republic. In the same year Philip's new governor, Alexander Farnese, reunited much of the Catholic south and east for Spain. In 1581 the northern provinces declared their independence, and William was elected *stadhouder* of the new Republic of the North (north of the river Rhine). In 1584 he was assassinated by a Catholic fanatic, hired by Spain. Under his son Maurice and Jan van Oldenbarneveldt, however, the rebels regained lost ground.

The conflict dragged on until 1648, when Spain finally acknowledged the sovereignty of the Republic of the North in the Treaty of Münster. It was agreed in principle that Catholic worship would be allowed in the Republic (although in practice open Catholic worship was not allowed and Catholicism was not formally recognized). The Catholic south remained loyal to Spain, and would later become Belgium. During the course of the revolt, as much as 10 percent of the population of the more highly developed south moved to the northern provinces.

The Golden Age

During the seventeenth century, the Netherlands became one of the world's greatest trading nations. It acquired a vast overseas empire through its power at sea, and Amsterdam overtook Antwerp as the center of international trade. As the economy thrived, so did cultural activity. This is the era of the great Dutch scholars, philosophers, jurists, bankers, engineers, and scientists. In 1625 the exiled Humanist Huig de Groot (Hugo Grotius) wrote *On the Law of War and Peace*, laying the foundations of international law. He also wrote about the freedom of the seas and international trade. Artists such as

Rembrandt, Frans Hals, Steen, and Vermeer broke with "classicism" in painting and changed the way we view the world. The Netherlands became the powerhouse of change— exporting ideas, skills, technology, capital, and enterprise. In a real sense it propelled Europe into the modern age.

The economy of the Dutch Republic was given a huge boost by the formation of the great trading companies. The Dutch United East India Company (Vereenigde Oost-Indische Compagnie, or VOC), founded in 1602, maintained its own fighting ships to defend its merchant vessels and its own army to protect its colonies and settlements. The Dutch West India Company was formed in 1621. It traded mainly in slaves, who were brought from Africa to America to work on the new plantations. Colonies were established in the Dutch East Indies (Indonesia), Dutch Guiana, on the northeastern coast of South America (Suriname), the Netherlands Antilles in the Caribbean, and at the Cape of Good Hope, on the southern tip of Africa. During the early 1600s there was a fierce struggle for economic supremacy between the Netherlands and England, which culminated in the wars of 1652–4 and 1664–7.

New York and the Dutch

In 1609 Henry Hudson, the English explorer commissioned by the Dutch East India Company to look for a western passage to India, sailed into New York Bay and up the Hudson River. The Netherlands claimed the territory, and established a colony and trading post at New Amsterdam, later managed by the Dutch West India Company. New Amsterdam was lost to Britain in 1664 in the course of the second Anglo–Dutch War, when it was exchanged for Suriname, and was subsequently christened New York in honor of the Duke of York.

After the treaty with Spain in 1648, there was a struggle for political power within the Dutch Republic between the Stadhouder, William II, and the regents of the individual States of the Republic. William, who was married to Mary Stuart, the daughter of Charles II of England, wanted to support the royalist cause in the English Civil War. The States did not want to be involved—it was expensive and not good for trade. Later on, in 1677, William III married another Mary Stuart, James II's daughter. He was offered the English throne in 1689 by the Whig opponents of James, who feared that he was about to reintroduce Roman Catholicism. As both Stadhouder and King of England, William was able to harmonize the colonial and commercial policies of the two countries. In 1674 the office of Stadhouder became hereditary in the Orange family. William III died in 1702.

French Rule

From 1689 to 1713, the Dutch and the English formed a coalition against the ambitions of Louis

XIV of France. The wars against France, which ended with the signing of the Treaty of Utrecht in 1713, took a heavy toll on Dutch finances. As a result England came to rule the trade routes formerly dominated by the Dutch, and became the leading commercial and industrial power. Exhausted, the Netherlands went into decline.

After the death of William IV in 1751 democratic ideas began spreading through the country. A group named the Patriots called for democratic constitutional reforms and limitations to the Stadhouder's powers. The Patriots were inspired by the colonial rebellion in America. Their more radical members drew up a constitution based upon the American Declaration of Independence.

William V defeated the Patriots in the 1780s with the help of his brother-in-law, the King of Prussia. However, they returned in 1795 with the French Revolutionary army and were welcomed by the populace. William went into exile. The radicals renamed the Dutch Republic the Batavian Republic. They instituted the separation of Church and State, guaranteed freedom of worship, and granted all religions legal equality.

In 1806 Napoleon made his brother Louis Bonaparte king, transforming the Batavian Republic into the Kingdom of Holland. Louis established his court in Amsterdam, which became the capital. He was actually a rather benevolent ruler, who started to keep some of the taxes for himself and allowed the Dutch to contravene some of the Imperial orders. He was removed from his position in 1810. However, Napoleon's defeat at Leipzig in 1813 spelled the collapse of his power outside France, and he withdrew his troops from the

Netherlands. Supporters of the House of Orange took power, declared a constitutional monarchy, and invited the heir to the House of Orange (the son of William V) back to the country. He was crowned King William I in 1814.

Independence

In the post-Napoleonic settlement at the Congress of Vienna in 1815, the seventeen states of the former "Seventeen United Netherlands" were reunited under the restored House of Orange. They did not stay united for long. After two and a half centuries of separation the differences in religion, culture, language, politics, and economics had become far too wide. In 1830, the dissatisfied Southerners seceded—with British and French help—and formed the independent state of Belgium. In 1839, after several years of negotiation, William finally confirmed the separation of Belgium and the northern Netherlands became known as the Kingdom of the Netherlands.

During his reign William did much to improve the economy of the Netherlands and to try to create a unified Dutch culture. In 1840, he abdicated in order to marry a Belgian Roman Catholic countess. He was succeeded by his son, William II, and died just three years later.

In 1848, in order to secure his position in the face of the rising tide of liberalism within Europe, William II agreed to constitutional changes that increased parliamentary democracy and subordinated the monarchy to a directly elected government. This still forms the basis of Dutch government today. On William's death in 1849 the throne passed to his son, William III.

The 1870s saw a rise in the fortunes of the Netherlands. New industries thrived and the country began to reap the benefits of industrial progress. The Dutch colonial empire in the East was strengthened. Increased prosperity had a positive effect upon culture and the arts, too.

William III died in 1890 and his daughter

Wilhelmina, who was only ten years old at the time, ascended to the throne. The Netherlands entered the twentieth century on a high note. Although it was no longer the force in Europe that it had been, there was pride in the developments at home and in its renewed status as a trading nation.

The Second World War (1939–45)
The country had remained neutral during the First World War, and was determined to stay out of the

Second World War. The majority of the population was pacifist, there was no army to speak of, and a great deal of its trade was with Germany. However, Germany invaded the Netherlands on May 10, 1940. Rotterdam was heavily bombed. Within five days the Dutch army was overwhelmed. The Dutch Resistance movement went underground, and Queen Wilhelmina rallied the people from London by broadcasting over the BBC.

During the German occupation 100,000 Jews were deported from the Netherlands and killed in concentration camps. More would have been deported had not ordinary Dutch families hidden them. Many people suffered extreme deprivation, especially in the last year of the war when food was scarce and the winter was hard. Dutch men were also taken to work in factories in Germany. The Allied forces liberated the Netherlands on April 29, 1945, and the war ended on May 5.

The Colonies

The Dutch East Indies were occupied by the Japanese during the war. At the end of the war, the colony renamed itself Indonesia and declared independence. Many people from the former Dutch colony moved to the Netherlands, which did not accept the independence of Indonesia until 1949.

Dutch Guiana became fully independent from the Netherlands as Suriname in 1975. Up to 1981, it was possible for Surinamers to choose between Surinamese or Dutch nationality. About 10,000 chose to take Dutch nationality.

The Netherlands Antilles ceased to exist in 2010, but the islands that formed it are now designated as either "autonomous countries" (Aruba, Curacao, and St. Maarten), or "autonomous special municipalities" (Bonaire, St Eustatius, and Saba), all within the Kingdom of the Netherlands.

Postwar Revival

The Netherlands was left in tatters by the war. It had to rebuild its economy and attend to the social needs of the people. America's Marshall Plan injected the finances and the Dutch tackled the problems with their customary vigor. In 1948 the Netherlands formed the Benelux customs union with Belgium

and Luxembourg. In the same year Queen Wilhelmina, who had returned after the war, abdicated after nearly sixty years on the throne, and her daughter Juliana succeeded her.

In 1949 the Netherlands became a founding member of NATO. Trade and industry revived, helped by the wealth brought through the discovery of natural gas fields in the North Sea. Unemployment fell so dramatically that there was a shortage of labor and thousands of migrants were welcomed into the country from Italy, Spain, Germany, Greece, Turkey, and Morocco. These people joined immigrants from the former Dutch East Indies, the Antilles, and Suriname to create an increasingly multicultural society.

In 1958, the Netherlands became a founding member of the European Economic Community. The increased prosperity that resulted from economic recovery enabled the government to address many social problems and a number of social programs were introduced. The paternalistic Dutch welfare system was established.

A Time for Change
The 1960s saw the start of widespread change. An anarchist group called the Provos was formed in Amsterdam, with the express intention of undermining authority. At first they did not enjoy public support. However, attitudes changed in 1965 when police set upon protesters in a needlessly brutal manner. The media questioned the way that the authorities were handling the matter, and members of the public raised concerns. Add to this the growing impact of television and the gradual breakdown of "pillarization" (see pages 39–40), and it is little wonder that a sea change took place. Perhaps because Dutch society had been so rigidly confined, the generation that emerged in the 1960s

took the opposite stance and became extremely liberal. At the same time, there was no Dutch secular conservative political party to challenge the dramatic changes. Liberal laws on soft drugs, homosexuality, abortion, divorce, prostitution, and euthanasia were swept through on the tide of change.

In the early 1980s unemployment rose and attitudes began to harden against people who were taking unfair advantage of the generous welfare system. Questions also began to be asked about the number of immigrants and asylum seekers entering the country, and the lack of integration of some sections of the immigrant community.

The Twenty-First Century
The Netherlands entered the twenty-first century with a buoyant economy. Unemployment had fallen dramatically and businesses were thriving. However, after the tragic events of September 11, 2001, the economy slowed down. In 2004 the extension of the EU into Eastern Europe led to an influx of workers from the new member countries, putting pressure on the Dutch labor market. A later economic boom gave way to yet another period of economic decline, from 2008 to 2014, during which time the government introduced austerity budgets that saw drastic cuts in public and social services. The sharp increase in immigration from Middle Eastern and African countries caused by the refugee crisis of 2015 was seen by many as exacerbating the social and financial pressures, and led to an erosion of confidence in the established political parties. This was compounded by the growth of Islamic militant extremism and terrorist acts in

Western Europe, which many people linked to open European Union borders. These concerns gave rise to a populist movement in the Netherlands that is anti-immigration, anti-Islam, and anti continued membership of the European Union, which are all deemed to be contrary to the national interest.

In spite of the economic recovery since 2014—which provides most Dutch people with a comfortable and happy lifestyle—times are unsettled. The 2017 general elections showed a country splintered in its views on how to approach the challenges of the day. However, the Dutch electorate stopped short of electing a right-wing populist party to become the leading party of the coalition and expressed a desire to remain in the European Union. The election result was regarded as a victory for moderation and the traditional Dutch approach.

CITIES IN THE NETHERLANDS

Each of the Netherlands' twelve provinces has its own capital. The greatest population growth centers around urban areas, particularly in the Randstad conglomeration of Amsterdam, Rotterdam, The Hague, and Utrecht. This is the commercial hub of the country, although many other large towns and cities have attracted industry, following improvements in communications technology and the transportation network.

The Hague

Until 1806, The Hague (Den Haag) was the capital of the Netherlands, although it had never been

granted city status. The Stadhouder, William II, the
Count of Holland, built a castle for himself there
in 1250. In 1511, the High Court of Holland was
established in The Hague, which became recognized
as the administrative and judicial center of the
Netherlands. Later, in 1578, The Hague also became
the seat of government when the States-General
began to hold its meetings there. When the House of
Orange became the royal family in 1814 their official
residence remained at The Hague. By this time,
however, Amsterdam had become the capital.

When Napoleon sent his brother Louis Bonaparte
to govern the Netherlands in 1806, Louis established
his court in the more worldly Amsterdam, which he
made the capital, although he did grant The Hague
city status by way of compensation.

Nowadays, The Hague is the third-largest city
in the Netherlands, with a population of about

526,000. It is the seat of government and the official residence of King Willem-Alexander. The Binnenhof (Inner Court) and Buitenhof (Outer Court) are the two chambers of Parliament, and the Ridderzaal (Knight's Hall, a restored thirteenth-century building) is used for ceremonial occasions, such as the delivery of the King's Speech each September.

The International Court of Justice and the Academy of International Law are also in The Hague, as are many of the foreign embassies. It is a refined, elegant, and cultured city, well worth a visit for its museums, art galleries, and upscale shops.

Amsterdam

The capital of the Netherlands, Amsterdam has a population of 850,000, although if you include the surrounding satellite communities and suburbs the figure is in the region of 1.1 million. It is the

largest Dutch city and the financial center of the country. It is also one of the key cultural centers and a big draw for tourists. It has a beautiful canal circle (the *grachten gordel*) dating from the start of the seventeenth century. It is famous for its cultural heritage, and there are excellent theaters, concert halls, museums, and art galleries to be found. Last but not least, Amsterdam is world-famous for its red-light district and for its "coffee shops," where soft drugs are sold for personal use. The city is an exotic blend of people from different backgrounds with a lively and fascinating mixture of subcultures.

Rotterdam

The second-largest city is Rotterdam, with a population of around 650,000. At the start of the Second World War, the Germans bombed Rotterdam and razed it to the ground as a warning to the Dutch of what would happen if they did not submit to

German occupation. After the war Rotterdam was rebuilt as a modern industrial and commercial city, and the largest port in the world. It is now renowned for its architecture and its unique atmosphere—modern and vibrant, with economic and commercial muscle but a cultural heart.

THE ROYAL FAMILY

In 2013 Queen Beatrix, who had reigned for thirty years, abdicated to enjoy her retirement years and her eldest son, Willem-Alexander, succeeded her. The Dutch generally regard their royal family with affection and respect. They are proud that their royals are informal. The premise of "*Doe maar gewoon . . .*" (see page 53) also applies to the royal family. Although they occasionally receive some criticism and scandals do occur, the Dutch royal family continues to be held in high regard.

GOVERNMENT

The Netherlands is a constitutional monarchy. There are three levels of government—central, provincial, and local. Central government, based at The Hague, is responsible for overseeing the other two levels. The King confirms the prime minister and plays an active part in forming the cabinet. The historical name for the parliament is the States-General (Staten-Generaal). This has two chambers—the First Chamber (Eerste Kamer) and the Second Chamber (Tweede Kamer). The country's twelve provincial councils indirectly elect members for a four-year period to the seventy-five seats in the First Chamber. This has a controlling function. It can ask the heads of the ministries and the state secretaries to explain their policies. It also has the right to carry out investigations.

The Second Chamber has a hundred and fifty seats. Its members, too, are elected for a four-year term. Its main function is legislation—proposing new laws and suggesting amendments to existing laws. If a bill is accepted by a majority of both chambers, the government is obliged to enact it.

Both bodies have representatives from the main political parties. In the Second Chamber, the allocation of seats is determined by the percentage of the total vote that each party receives—a system of proportional representation. Votes are cast for political policies, not for individuals, and representatives are chosen according to their position on the party list, not for their personal qualities. They do not represent a particular area or constituency.

The large number of political parties makes it difficult to form a government. In order to obtain a reasonable number of seats and to increase their influence in the Second Chamber some of the historical political parties have united to form new larger parties. Dutch governments are usually a coalition of two or three parties.

Today there are such wide differences between the political parties on key issues, such as immigration or the extent of involvement with the European Union, that it is increasingly difficult for them to come to an agreement and form a coalition. The negotiation process seems to take longer after each general election, which means that the practical business of government can be suspended in limbo for months at time, with ministers from the outgoing administration performing a holding function.

LIVING APART TOGETHER

The term "Pillarization" (*Versuiling*) describes a peculiarly Dutch arrangement—the segregation of society along political and religious lines. In the late nineteenth century Dutch society split into distinct sections or communities. Each of these groups (or "pillars") had its own religion, schools, media, political party, and even sports clubs. Within each pillar there were different social levels—workers and professional classes, religious and political leaders—although the contribution of all individuals to the success of the community was acknowledged.

The idea was to "live apart together." The sections of society were separate but seen as contributing to the common interest of the country as a whole. Imagine a classical building with a roof held up by separate columns, using their combined strength to support it. For this system to work, political leaders had to seek a consensus in order to make a decision.

In the 1960s the old system of "pillarization" began to break down. People became exposed to other ideas through the media, and gradually the barriers between different communities were eroded. At the same time the Dutch became more aware of political movements outside the country, which also influenced public opinion.

In the 1970s and '80s, a different type of "living apart together" was created when growing numbers of immigrants began to enter the Netherlands. Separate communities of different races settled in particular areas. Some kept to their traditional way of life and culture as best as they could. Dutch law enabled and even encouraged this voluntary segregation by making it possible for these communities to set up their own schools, in which children could be taught the cultural norms and values of their original, rather than their adopted, country. Concerns started to surface in the 1980s and '90s that instead of the immigrants integrating into Dutch society, in some parts of the Netherlands Dutch culture was gradually being displaced by that of the new arrivals.

An attempt was made to address these concerns. In the 1990s laws were introduced to ensure that foreigners coming to settle long-term in the Netherlands learned the Dutch language and culture, in order to be able to contribute to the economy as quickly as possible. However, the issue of immigration did not go away and it resurfaced when it was taken up by a new arrival on the political stage—Pim Fortuyn.

PIM FORTUYN

In 2001 Pim Fortuyn swept on to the political scene. He decried the constant discussion and debate strangling Dutch politics. He wanted politicians to tackle major issues in a practical manner, particularly transport and health care, and to stop papering over the cracks between parties in the coalition. He declared that the Dutch were no longer prepared to put up with the official levels of tolerance imposed by law to protect the rights of minorities. Most people were appalled. He was likened to Jean-Marie Le Pen, and even to Mussolini. The party that had chosen him as its leader—Leefbaar Nederland (Livable Netherlands)— dropped him after he made racist remarks in an interview. Undeterred, he went ahead to form his own party—Lijst Pim Fortuyn (LPF). He was in the middle of a colorful election campaign when an animal rights activist assassinated him in May 2002.

No public figure had been killed in the Netherlands since 1584 and the Dutch were shocked. They regarded it as an attack upon democracy itself, and on the right of people to speak their mind. Fortuyn's political party received over a million votes in the general election after his murder. Some commentators saw this extraordinary result as a protest by a section of society against the killing of a public figure, not as support for his views.

Others interpreted it as a clear indication that public opinion was starting to turn against the Dutch tradition of tolerance.

THE RISE OF POPULISM

In 2006 Geert Wilders stepped into the space left by the death of Pim Fortuyn. Wilders claimed—as had Pim Fortuyn before him—to be speaking for ordinary people against the political elite. In the 2010 general elections Wilder's party (the PVV—Freedom Party) rose in popularity with an anti-immigration, anti-Islam, and anti-European Union agenda. The strength of support for the PVV was seen as a reflection of the Dutch population's frustration with their traditional political parties and with the leadership of the European Union.

However, many Dutch people regard Wilder's behavior as inflammatory. In 2016 he was found guilty of "group insult" and of "inciting discrimination" at a rally in 2014. Surprise was expressed that he received no punishment. In fact, his party's popularity continued to rise. Austerity cuts during the recession had affected many of the poorer groups in Dutch society and some felt that refugees were putting an already stretched social welfare system under far too much pressure. In the months before the 2017 elections, the PVV, with Wilders at its helm, was running ahead in the polls. It looked as if the PVV would become the party with the largest share of support from the Dutch voting public, but this was not to be. Eighty percent of the electorate voted in the March 2017 general elections and the moderate majority prevailed. The PVV did get over 13 percent of the vote, with 20 of the 150 seats in the lower house, but the center-right Liberal VVD (People's Party for Freedom and Democracy) pulled out in front and took 33 of the seats.

All the parties that won seats in the 2017 elections made it clear that they would not form a coalition with the PVV. Wilders has called the move "undemocratic" and an insult to the people who voted for his party. He continues to take any opportunity to cross swords with the established parties, and to make statements calculated to promote his party's policies and to cause a stir. He is not going to go away, and the other politicians will have to deal with him and his influence on the Dutch electorate.

THE DUTCH IN THE EU

The Netherlands was one of the founding members of the European Union. After the Second World War there was a move toward greater European integration. In May 1948, Princess Juliana and Prince Bernhard hosted the Congress of Europe in The Hague. This was the first step on the road to a European Union. In 1952, six European countries— the Netherlands, Belgium, France, Germany, Italy, and Luxembourg—combined to form the European Coal and Steel Community (ECSC) to bring the industries under common control for economic and security reasons. In 1958, the Dutch Minister of Foreign Affairs played an important role in setting up the European Economic Community (EEC).

The Netherlands has been keen from the start to have an influence on the ideas, policies, and laws to emerge from the Union, especially with regard to commercial and social issues. In 1967, the ECSC, the EEC, and the European Atomic Energy Community joined together to form the European Communities (EC). In 1973, three more countries joined the EC, including Britain, and more have joined since then.

The Maastricht Summit, held in the Netherlands in 1991, was crucial in laying the foundations for economic and monetary union. When the Maastricht Treaty came into force in 1993, the EC became the European Union. As a trading nation, the Netherlands has supported the creation of a single market and the removal of trade barriers. As a small country within Europe, it has regarded the EU as a security measure—ensuring that the interests of the larger states do not override the concerns of smaller ones. The EU gives the Netherlands a voice and representation in a body that has a common purpose, and ensures that national interests do not overwhelm the common interest of its members.

The Netherlands is also a member of the Eurozone—the Dutch guilder has been replaced by the euro—which is an indication of the level of its commitment to the EU. However, the Netherlands has not totally embedded itself in Europe. It also keeps an eye on the Atlantic and takes note of what is happening in America and other parts of the world. As a trading nation, it needs to keep a finger on the pulse of events in all four corners of the globe.

Events early in the twenty-first century reduced confidence for some in the policy making and decision-making of the European leaders. In 2004 the EU admitted a number of central and eastern European countries, with a resulting westward migration of new EU citizens. Many of these people moved back to their own countries after just a few years, but it did lead to a fear across Europe of the potential erosion of national cultures. This was further exacerbated by the huge influx of immigrants, primarily from the Middle East and Africa, in the summer of 2015, part of the largest migration across Europe since the end of the Second World War. Many people in the Netherlands questioned the EU's handling of the situation, and calls increased for closed borders to regain control of population movement and to reduce the number of terrorist attacks by Islamic extremist groups.

In June 2016, the British voted to leave the European Union—"Brexit"—and in November 2016 the populist, anti-establishment businessman and TV celebrity, Donald Trump, was elected president of the United States. These events were interpreted by the media as part of a wider populist trend, which members of the European Commission feared could lead to the eventual disintegration of the European Union. The Dutch general elections in March 2017 were watched closely as an indication of what might happen in the upcoming French and German elections. There was huge relief when the Dutch did not give as large a portion of the vote as expected to the PVV. This was regarded as a win for the moderate majority and a reprieve for the European Union, as it was hoped that French and German voters would follow suit and reaffirm faith in, and stabilize, the EU position. Sure enough, in June 2017 the French rejected Marine le Pen's far-right Front National party and elected a centrist government under President Macron, and in Germany in September 2017 Angela Merkel's center-right CDU/CSO party was reelected, albeit with a reduced majority.

Generally the Dutch believe strongly in the need for the controlling influence of international law. They recognize the reality of American power, but consider it essential for all NATO members to ensure that they use their power justly and correctly. They value the principles of order, restraint, and justice, and they are not averse to pointing out to other countries, no matter how big and powerful, the error of their ways.

THE DUTCH PEOPLE TODAY

Since the start of the twenty-first century the rise of populism and associated nationalism has led to a resolve on the part of some to reaffirm traditional Dutch standards, customs, and values. Although the call for immigrants to assimilate into Dutch culture has increased, there are also many Dutch people who continue to welcome multiculturalism and believe that "living apart together" still works well to maintain harmony in a diverse and pluralistic country. (See "pillarization" on page 39.)

Although the 2008–14 recession in the Netherlands increased the number of people living on the poverty line and created a greater divide between rich and poor, the vast majority of Dutch people enjoy a comfortable lifestyle and a good work/life balance. A UNICEF report in 2013 identified Dutch children as being the happiest in the world. Of course there are always new challenges to be met. As a trading nation, the Netherlands faces changes as a result of Brexit and the Trump administration's policies, and it will need to adapt accordingly, making the most of any opportunities that arise to consolidate its recently improved economic position. It will also need to face up to the divisions within Dutch society and try to minimize any resentment and conflict inherent within these—for example, the growing gap between the lifestyles of wealthy and poorer Dutch citizens, and the divisions between native Dutch and immigrants from different cultures, with traditions and values that are perceived to conflict with the Dutch way of life. There is a rising tide of anti-Islamic feeling.

Some sections of Dutch society, of course, have always lived by traditional values and continue to do so. In the next chapter we look in greater depth at what those values are.

VALUES & ATTITUDES

THE INFLUENCE OF CALVIN

Much has been made of the fact that Dutch society is
built upon Calvinist ethics and values. For the most
part, today this is a secularized version of Calvinism.
People believe in the value of debate, and the right of
individuals to express their opinion before decisions
are reached. They live in modest homes, which they
make cozy in order to be happy. They do not spend
large sums of money, and if they do they tend to
keep it quiet. How do these aspects of Dutch life
stem from Calvinist teachings?

The strict and uncompromising ideas of the
French theologian and reformer John Calvin

(1509–64) became
increasingly popular in the
Netherlands from 1560
onward. He preached that
God determined peoples'
fate; therefore, they should
know and accept their place
in the world and not try to
rise above it. All people were
equal and material wealth
or status meant nothing in
religious terms. As men were

born with Original Sin, according to Calvin, they should strive to improve themselves and to help others, so that God would forgive them. This formed the religious basis for a social conscience.

Calvin believed that the judgment of others was worthwhile if it corresponded with God's purpose and helped individuals both to see the error of their ways and to keep in line with moral requirements.

He taught that it was necessary to be sober in lifestyle, to be stoical, and to accept what life brought. People should put effort into using the talents that God had given them wisely, but not expect congratulations for their achievements, for they would prosper only if it were God's will that they should do so. As  a trained lawyer, Calvin presented his ideas in a forceful, rational, and well-argued manner.

The Dutch had a choice between Calvinism and Lutheranism, which was a less strict form of Protestantism. Lutheranism may have been rejected because it was more tolerant of many traditional Catholic practices. The merchants regarded it as unfair to be toiling in order to line the pockets of the Church. They also resented the payment of exorbitant taxes to the Catholic King of Spain.

The majority of the merchant class chose Calvinism. The very fact that it was harsh could have been its main appeal: God was seen as a punishing rather than a benevolent and nurturing deity. The vast majority of Dutch people in the sixteenth century lived hard lives, battling for survival against the constant threat of floods and weather, and perhaps they could identify in this the hand of an uncompromising God.

Calvinism probably also appealed to the Dutch because they were a nation of traders and merchants. The wealthy burghers were attracted by a religion that told people to accept their lot and be content with their position in society. They were at the top of the pecking order, and any doctrine that helped preserve their position in society was bound to be well received.

Interestingly, the Calvinist ethos still holds sway today, even though there are currently more Catholics than Protestants in the Netherlands, of whom only a small portion are Calvinists. In the four and a half centuries that have passed since the emergence of Dutch Calvinism, many of its values have become embedded in Dutch society as a whole.

Calvinist rigor has been tempered by the Humanism of Erasmus, who believed in the intrinsic goodness of humankind and the need for humane and nonviolent behavior in the resolution of disputes. This combination of Calvinist and Humanist values lies at the heart of key institutions in the Netherlands, such as the government, and informs the laws of the land. It would require a revolution in Dutch society to pry it out and replace it with something else. On the whole, the Dutch are proud of their values and are in no hurry to change them. They provide stability and continuity in a changing world. Although the rise of public concern over immigration to the Netherlands has put some of these traditional values under strain in recent years, they continue to be held by the majority of the population. At the core of Dutch values is a respect for others and the desire to live in harmony.

EGALITARIANISM AND DEMOCRACY

The Dutch consider it very important that all citizens have equal rights. In practical terms, this means constant consultation with representatives from each section of the community. Many local meetings are held to try to take everyone's requirements and opinions into account. This can prove very difficult when the opinions being expressed are extremely diverse.

The dominant way of living in the Netherlands is *samenleving* (living together), and that means individuals fitting in with and caring about society as a whole. Active citizenship underpins Dutch society. In the Netherlands, people not only have a right to get involved, but they also have a duty to do so. As a result, children are taught to express their opinions and to feel that they have a right to be heard. This prepares them to become the sort of adults who will participate well in Dutch society, taking advantage of the opportunities given to express their views and to influence the decisions that affect daily life.

NATIONAL PRIDE

The Dutch are a proud nation, and justifiably so. As a local saying goes, "God made the Earth, but the Dutch made Holland." They have conquered the sea, in order to make the best use of the area available to them, and their engineers have an excellent reputation throughout the world. The nation may be small but it is one of the wealthiest in the world, and even during the recent economic downturn the Dutch continued to enjoy a relatively high standard of living. They are also renowned for their ability in trade and the success of their commercial maritime empire. At times, however, this pride can seem to outsiders to have a rather arrogant and judgmental tone—the Dutch know best. There is a propensity to give advice when it has not been asked for, but they are usually quite happy for you to disagree and to argue back. In fact, they respect people for sticking up for their own point of view and admire a well-argued case.

ADDED VALUE AND THRIFT

The Dutch are resourceful, and the recycling of goods (as well as of paper, glass, compost, and so on) is an integral part of Dutch life. Until recently, any unwanted large items could be left out on the sidewalk for vans to collect. One would often see people sorting through the rubbish—it was perfectly acceptable to take something, after having checked with the original owner. Sidewalk collections are not so common now, but the same process takes place in the local *kringloopcentrum* (recycling center), where all the larger items are gathered to sell to new owners.

WORK ETHIC AND MODESTY

The Dutch are diligent and hard workers, although they believe that you should "work to live and not live to work". However, during the 2008–14 recession some people struggled to maintain their former standard of living and had to put in more hours at work, at the expense of time normally devoted to family and other interests.

The general Dutch standard of living remains comfortable, but talking about personal finances is usually regarded as unacceptable, and ostentatious behavior is discouraged, certainly by the older generation. For the majority of Dutch people improving your lot is about spending more time and sharing activities with family or friends, or in achieving personal goals, rather than about acquiring extra things and proving your success to others.

"DOE MAAR GEWOON . . ."

"Doe maar gewoon, want gewoon is gek genoeg!" means "Behave normally, that's strange enough!" Underlying this expression is the Dutch spirit of egalitarianism and conformity—nobody is better than anybody else and should not think that they are. It is unacceptable to try to get yourself noticed, because setting yourself apart from other people implies that you are superior in some way. In this respect, the Dutch are somewhat more conformist than the Americans or British.

The point is to fit in with, and blend into, society. At first, this appears to be at odds with the renowned Dutch tolerance of diversity. These two apparently opposing principles can operate in harmony. While all manner of views and behavior are tolerated, it is expected that individuals will not impose the ideas of their group on others. Many Dutch people abide by traditional norms of behavior. Those outside are free to choose their way of life, as long as it doesn't encroach upon or cause any threat to society as a whole.

The principle of "living apart together" has enabled different sections of Dutch society to tolerate each other from a distance for a number of years. However, some people are no longer as supportive of the principle as they used to be. They consider that foreigners living in the Netherlands should be forced to integrate much more and "*doe maar gewoon*" to avoid the gradual erosion of Dutch values and culture.

The Prime Minister, Mark Rutte, added to this debate with an open letter just before the 2017 general elections. In his letter he called for people to "*normaal doen*" (behave normally) and fit in with Dutch values and traditions of behavior, or to "*ga het land uit*" (leave the country). Critics commented that the letter was targeted at foreigners living in the country and it was felt by some to exacerbate the divisions. Other people agreed with his sentiments, and his level of popularity proved to be higher than expected at the elections, where his party received the largest mandate.

Although Dutch laws are liberal, it would be naive to assume that this broadmindedness extends to all towns within the provinces. Generally speaking, the more rural the area, the more conservative the people.

Also you need to be aware that a few areas of the country still have a high percentage of strictly religious people, and liberal views are not so easily tolerated in such communities.

STOICISM

The older Dutch generation was shaped by the hardship of the German occupation in the Second World War, and has little time for anybody who complains about minor problems or difficulties. The younger generations have been raised to dust themselves off and get on with things in a positive and pragmatic manner. Don't moan! Emotions such as depression or grief are generally regarded as private matters and are usually only expressed within the immediate family or among close friends. Over effusiveness is similarly regarded with a degree of distrust—as an indication of insincerity and superficiality, rather than as a genuine expression of pleasure. The Dutch do, of course, express joy and have fun times—stoicism does not preclude appreciating life.

CLEANLINESS AND HEALTH

Many Dutch houses are very clean, tidy, and well maintained—outside as well as inside. Cleanliness is an ingrained value that holds good for the majority of Dutch people. Its origins lie in the Calvinist belief that cleanliness is next to godliness, and the idea that people who are gainfully employed in housework are not wasting time on idle chatter or other mischief.

Nowadays religious belief is not so widespread, but keeping one's home clean and tidy is still regarded as important. It is a way of providing the family with a healthy and happy environment.

DUTCH HONESTY

Many people are struck by the forthright nature of the Dutch. As we have seen, they are positively encouraged from childhood to voice their opinions. This spills over into personal exchanges, and can be hard to handle if taken as criticism, rather than as a comment. They also prefer you to tell them what you really think, and are wary of what they regard as excessive politeness. Generally speaking, they do not say "please" quite as often as English-speakers do, and if they want something their request can sound rather abrupt to foreign ears. However, they do lay great store on saying "thank you" (*dank je wel* in the familiar form, or *dank u wel* in the polite form) and respond with "you're welcome" (*alsjeblieft* or *alstublieft*) when they have done something for you, whatever that is.

The middle-aged and elderly Dutch can be wary of overfamiliarity from people who do not know them well. You might feel as if you are being held at arm's length, in a polite but slightly reserved manner. The right to be regarded as a friend has to be earned. Once this has been achieved, your Dutch friends will be extremely loyal to you and will help you out in any way that they can when you are in need. Younger people are more open to casual friendships and are often much less reserved.

Be Yourself

A British woman visiting a Dutch friend was offered a cup of coffee. "*Ja graag*" ("Yes please"), she replied. Upon being offered milk and sugar she answered in the same manner, and again, when offered a cookie she said "Thank you" ("*Dank je wel*"). Her Dutch friend told her she didn't have to say please and thank you all the time—a straight "yes" or "no" would do fine after the first "please"! The visitor replied that her manners were part of her upbringing, and not something she was willing to alter in order to fit in. The Dutch woman accepted this explanation with a smile, and her guest's "excessive" politeness was never remarked upon again.

GEZELLIGHEID

The feeling of *gezelligheid* is central to Dutch social life. The dictionary defines *gezellig* as "cozy," but "congenial" is possibly more accurate, describing a situation or atmosphere that is relaxed, positive, and full of fellow feeling.

Gezelligheid is about people enjoying themselves in the company of others—it is not really about solitary pleasures. If a Dutch person tells you that time spent with you was *gezellig*, you can take it that they enjoyed themselves and felt relaxed and at ease in your company—a compliment!

COMMUNITY SPIRIT

Gezelligheid is also related to being sociable and living harmoniously with others—getting along well. Conformity to social rules is seen as the basis of security for all, and community spirit is an essential part of Dutch life. This manifests itself in the concern shown for vulnerable people in the community and the support available for them.

However, the downside of community spirit can be that neighbors feel free to comment if they consider that a local resident or group is letting their neighborhood down in any way. This could be about something as trivial as not keeping their garden tidy, or about more extreme behavior, such as creating a major disturbance with too much noise. In America or Britain this sort of intervention would probably be regarded as interference, but in the Netherlands it is an acceptable way of showing concern and maintaining social harmony. It is regarded by some as part of good citizenship.

People who prefer their own company and are unsociable may be accused of being *ongezellig*. If they decline to join in with communal activities— the idea being to have fun and enjoy things as part of a group, rather than as an individual—they are regarded as not playing a proper part in society. If you are not a naturally gregarious person, be prepared to put yourself out and participate in group activities if you want to be accepted by your Dutch acquaintances and friends.

Many Dutch people demonstrate their community spirit by working voluntarily for locally based organizations. Their contribution is valued and encouraged. Volunteers are organized through a central agency in each main town and prizes are awarded every year to people who have made exceptional contributions.

RELIGION

After the loss of the Catholic southern provinces, Calvinism predominated in the Netherlands. Although tolerated, other religions were not given equal rights until the late eighteenth century.

In the late nineteenth century there was a split within the Dutch Reformed Church (Nederlands Hervormde Kerk). The theologian and politician Abraham Kuyper (1837–1920) established the more strictly Calvinistic Gereformeerde Kerk (or Reformed Church). Kuypers considered that the national Dutch Reformed Church was far too liberal. He stood for a return to the strict teachings of the Reformation period. He promoted the idea that members of the new Reformed Church should isolate themselves from other communities, so that they would not be "besmirched" or influenced by other beliefs. This was the start of "pillarization" in Dutch society. Pillarization came to an end when religious belief began to decline and people realized that they could share political goals even if their religions were different. Thus the CDA (Christian

Democratic Appeal) is a fusion of a Catholic and two Calvinist political parties. Fewer people attend church nowadays, or belong to a particular religious community. Nevertheless, 56 percent of the population identifies with a religious faith.

There are, however, still certain parts of the country where the Gereformeerde Kerk is influential—in the so-called "Bible Belt," which takes

in a number of towns and villages in a diagonal line across the country, from Zeeland up to the northwest of the Overijssel province. Within the Bible Belt some people still dress in traditional costume and members of the Reformed Church embrace orthodox Calvinist doctrine. There, for example, it is unacceptable for people to work—to wash their windows, clean cars, or mow lawns—on a Sunday, which is reserved for religious devotion. The Calvinists have an extensive knowledge of the Bible and are expected to adhere to its teachings literally.

Members of the mainstream Protestant Hervormde Kerk have far more liberal views than members of the Gereformeerde Kerk. Catholics in the Netherlands tend to be less rigid on the whole than strict Roman Catholics elsewhere.

chapter three

CUSTOMS &
TRADITIONS

The Dutch celebrate a wide variety of national events. Some have religious origins, others historical significance. For the most part, they provide a great reason for having a party. The importance of communal life is reflected in people's pride in the larger community—the nation as a whole—and in their smaller communities—towns, villages, and neighborhoods. This pride and sense of belonging is demonstrated and shared through communal celebrations and having a *gezellig* time together.

NATIONAL FESTIVALS
National festivals provide an opportunity for visitors to mingle with the locals and share in the enjoyment. The following are the main events in the order that they occur during the year.

January 1—New Year's Day (Nieuwjaarsdag)
You can normally still hear fireworks going off on New Year's Day but nowhere near to the extent that they do on New Year's Eve! Many people

spend the day quietly after the celebrations the night before. It is often a time for people to get some fresh air and exercise by going out for a walk, cycling, or ice-skating if the weather is very cold.

February—Carnival (Carnaval)

This takes place on the weekend before Fat (Shrove) Tuesday and is celebrated by the Catholic communities. Everybody (children included) dresses up in wonderful bright costumes and takes part in parades. There is usually a huge party. Check out www.expatica.com/nl for a list of the major Dutch towns celebrating carnival each year.

April 1—April Fool's Day

Practical jokes are elevated to an art form. People play them on each other, and almost all the newspapers and Dutch television channels take part in the fun by covering a "story" that turns out later to be a hoax.

Media Fun
VPRO Radio (the Liberal Protestant Radio
network) once "covered" a strange affliction
that had struck Rembrandt's painting *The Night
Watch*. The paint had begun to peel off slowly
but surely, and the whole image was expected to
vanish by midnight. The National Gallery would
reopen at 8:00 p.m. so that art-lovers countrywide
could cast one last glance at the famous painting.
A considerable crowd gathered in front of the
museum. It was not until reporters from VPRO
Radio began to interview them that people caught
on that it was a gigantic April Fool's joke.

April—National Museum Week (Nationaal Museumweek)

This event is normally held early in April. Free
entry to many museums gives everybody the
chance to have a cultural day out, but do not expect
the main tourist museums in Amsterdam to be free.
Naturally, many people take advantage of this and
the museums are usually packed. You can find out
which week it is, plus what is going on and where,
at www.holland.com.

April 27—King's Day (Koningsdag)

This is a major holiday that takes place on April 27,
which is King Willem-Alexander's birthday. Red,
white, and blue national flags, and orange ensigns
for the House of Orange, festoon the houses.
Each year, as part of the festivities, the monarch
and his family pay an official visit to two towns,

where they are received with great acclaim. On Koningsdag many towns hold fairs, and the streets are full of families selling their secondhand goods, displayed on the ground on blankets, or on stands in the market squares. Children are out in force, too—selling their old toys or clothes, and playing musical instruments to earn a bit of money from passers-by. Everybody is dressed in orange clothes or wigs and great fun is had by all!

Late May/Early June—Flag Day and the First Herring Catch Auction

The town of Scheveningen is decorated, local people dress up in traditional costume, and the King is offered the *Koningsharing*—the best herring of the catch. The first barrel of herrings is auctioned off, with the proceeds going to charity.

National Windmill Day (Nationale Molendag)

National Windmill Day is normally held on either the second Saturday or Sunday in May. On this day many of the country's working windmills are open to the public with demonstrations and talks. See https://www.molens.nl/english/ for details.

November 11—St. Martin's Day (Sint Maarten's Dag)

Small groups of children carrying paper lanterns go from door to door in their local neighborhood (usually accompanied by a parent) to sing traditional St. Martin's Day songs in exchange for sweets and other treats such as fruit from their neighbors.

Mid November to early December—St. Nicholas (Sinterklaas)

The historical St. Nicholas (Sinterklaas) was Bishop of Myra in Lycia, in present-day Turkey, in the fourth century CE. The ancient celebration of his feast day was made optional by the Roman Catholic Church in 1968, although it was stressed that there was no doubt about his authenticity. St. Nicholas is known as the friend and protector of people in need. He is the patron saint of children, sailors, scholars, travelers, and merchants, to name but a few.

"Sinterklaas" arrives in Amsterdam on a boat from Spain with his Moorish servants—the Black Peters (*Zwarte Pieten*). He tours the country on a white horse, visiting all the main towns to the great excitement of the children. Some are in awe of him, because their parents tell them that he knows all about them—who has been good during the year and who has been bad.

The Zwarte Pieten throw cookies and sweets to the children and generally clown around, singing, or playing musical instruments. Children used to

be told that they would take naughty children away in their sacks and only give sweets to the good ones. This aspect is now played down, so as not to perpetuate racist stereotypes. The Zwarte Pieten are still mainly white people with their faces blackened to look like Moors, and this is accepted in many places as a part of tradition. For American and British visitors it can be a shock!

In August 2015 the UN Committee on the Elimination of Racial Discrimination wrote to the Dutch government expressing concerns about the negative racial stereotyping inherent in the Zwarte Pieten cultural tradition, which it warned contravened the human rights of racial minority groups. In recent years, there have also been a growing number of protests in the Netherlands against the perceived racism of the tradition. As a result, some of the main cities have introduced Zwarte Piets with sooty smears on their faces, rather than the usual complete blacking up. It has been suggested that this will gradually be introduced to more towns and cities and that there will also be more plain Piets with clean faces too.

Sinterklaas' birthday is celebrated by families, especially those with younger children, on December 5 with *pakjesavond* (present evening). On the days leading up to *pakjesavond* the children put out an empty shoe at night, and Sinterklaas leaves them a few chocolates or sweets. On *pakjesavond* itself, people give each other surprises, presents that are normally inexpensive but are chosen with care and cleverly wrapped to disguise the contents. They are given with a poem, supposedly penned by Sinterklaas and the Zwarte Pieten, that is a humorous portrait of the recipient's good points and weaknesses. These poems can be pretty sharp. They also often refer to activities that the recipient enjoys, and the "surprise" may be related to this activity—for example a papier-mâché mockup of a computer or a football. On December 6, Sinterklaas returns to Spain until the next year.

December 25 and 26—Christmas Day and Boxing Day (Eerste Kerstdag and Tweede Kerstdag)
These have traditionally been low-key occasions in comparison with Sinterklaas, with people attending church, having a Christmas tree, and exchanging cards and a few presents. They celebrate in a quiet manner within the family. The festival is now becoming more widely celebrated in a way that would feel familiar to the British and Americans.

December 31—New Year's Eve (Oud en Nieuw)
The New Year is celebrated by setting off thousands of fireworks at midnight. There are few organized

firework displays, other than in the larger cities. Fireworks can be ordered and collected from licensed businesses in the days running up to New Year's Eve, but it is illegal to set them off before the holiday itself. Not that this stops crowds of boys gathering on street corners and setting off chains of firecrackers!

Individuals at family gatherings light most of the fireworks between midnight and 1:00 a.m. on New Year's Eve/Day. Safety is not given a very high priority, and there are accidents each year, despite warnings on television. If you are at all worried it is best to stay and watch from indoors, although you will miss some of the atmosphere of the event. People gather on the street just after midnight (having first drunk a toast to their family members inside their houses) to shake hands and wish each other well for the year to come. It is a friendly atmosphere. Typical treats are *appelflappen*—fried battered apple rings—and *olliebollen*—a kind of doughnut filled with raisins.

ANNUAL SPECIAL EVENTS
A number of special events are held throughout the country on an annual basis. They include:

Late January/Early February: The International Film Festival, Rotterdam—quality independent films are shown in a number of venues around the city.

March: The European Fine Art Fair, Maastricht—a huge fine arts and antiques fair in south Limburg that attracts dealers from around the world.

Also, the opening of the famous Keukenhof Gardens near Lisse in South Holland.

April: The Flower Parade (Bloemencorso) takes place in the bulb-growing area between Haarlem and Noordwijk in the last week of April, with colorful floats and a parade.

Also, the World Press Photography Exhibition in Amsterdam runs from April until June/July.

May/June: Jazz and blues music festivals are held in many towns nationwide.

June: Pinkpop, an open-air pop and rock music festival held in Landgraaf, Limburg province.

June/July: The Holland Festival, held in Amsterdam with ballet, theater, opera, music, and film.

Also, the open-air Vondelpark Festival, with free performances of dance, children's theater, plays, and music in the park.

July: The North Sea Jazz Festival, held in The Hague. A big event, with internationally renowned jazz bands in open air performances throughout the city.

Also, the Rotterdam Summer Carnival (Zomercarnaval)— with a parade and Latin music.

End July/Early August: Gay Pride in Amsterdam— the week's events include the iconic Canal Parade.

August: Uitmarkt—free music and theater performances in Amsterdam to mark the end of one theater season and the start of the next.

Also, the Scheveningen International Fireworks Festival—magnificent displays on the beach as part of a firework display competition.

September: Flower Parade, taking place between Aalsmeer, where many of the flower auction houses are based, and Amsterdam, in early September, with colorful floats, bands, and drum majorettes.

Monument Day (Monumentendag), held on the second Saturday of the month. This is a chance to see inside historical buildings that are usually closed to the public.

November: The International Documentary Film Festival is held in Amsterdam for film fans and professionals.

There are many more special events on offer nationwide. The following Web sites are useful:
• www.expatica.com/nl/festivals-in-the-netherlands
• www.holland.com
• www.iamsterdam.com/en/visiting/whats-on/ festivals
• www.daysout.nl

FAMILY CELEBRATIONS

As we have seen, the family is important to the Dutch, and family celebrations are a time for everybody to get together (with their friends too) to relax and have some fun.

Birthdays

These are important occasions. Family and friends
get together at the home of the birthday person and
everyone brings a small present. It is not necessary to
give something expensive, but find out what they would
like by asking a close family member. A *verlanglijst*
(wish list) may have been compiled. The Dutch send
birthday cards only if they cannot attend the celebration
and many now send e-cards, or communicate with the
birthday person on social media.

Do learn to say "*Gefeliciteerd!*" If you are invited to
a birthday party, you will hear people congratulating
the birthday person, "*Gefeliciteerd met je verjaardag!*"
They will also congratulate everybody else present,
particularly the relatives of the person whose birthday
it is, but also most of the guests. "*Gefeliciteerd met de
verjaardag van je zoon!*" or "*je vrouw*" or "*je moeder.*"
("Congratulations on your son's birthday . . . your
wife's birthday . . . your mother's birthday.")

Birthday parties are normally an open-house event,
without formal invitations. If you have been before,
you are expected to come again. You may be asked
to come at a particular time—if you're not sure, ask
when would be most convenient for your host(ess).
Generally, guests arrive from about 10:00 a.m.
onward. You will be served coffee and cake or sweet
pastry. After two cups of coffee, you will be offered an
alcoholic or soft drink and savory snacks. Do not stay
all day, no matter how *gezellig* it is.

A fiftieth birthday is a special occasion. The
birthday person is traditionally said to have reached
the age of maturity and wisdom, and they are known
as a "Sarah" (women) or an "Abraham" (men). You

may see a large straw doll of a man or a woman in the front garden of a house with banners and flags proclaiming "*Gefeliciteerd Wout/Hennie — 50 vandaag!*"—"Congratulations Wout/Hennie— 50 today!" One-hundredth birthdays are also marked with great ceremony.

Weddings

These are also celebrated with gusto. In the Netherlands all weddings take place in the *gemeentehuis* (town hall) with a civic ceremony in order to be legally recognized. The couple can also choose to have a church service. There is often a celebration meal for members of the close family, and then a larger party or reception for other relatives, friends, and acquaintances. If you want to buy a gift for the happy couple, the invitation will include the name and telephone number or e-mail address of the *Ceremoniemeester* (Master of Ceremonies—usually a relative or good friend of the couple), who will have a gift list. If money is requested, put the check or cash into an envelope with a card and post it into the box provided at the reception.

At a larger party, it is usual for close relatives to have composed a song relating something funny about the couple and generally teasing them. There may be a homemade video in a similar vein.

Birth of a Baby

The birth of a baby is announced to the neighborhood. The front garden of the proud parents' home is decked out with pink or blue flags, balloons, a "washing line" with pink or blue doll's clothes, and a large cardboard stork with the baby's date of birth, name, and weight written on it. The parents will usually also send out announcement cards inviting family and friends to visit the new addition to the family within set times during the day, or by appointment. You should take a small gift for the baby—clothing, a photo album, or toy—and flowers for the mother. You will be given a cup of coffee or tea (which the Dutch drink weak with sugar, if required, but not with milk) and a *beschuit met muisjes*—a sort of rusk with tiny aniseed sweets in pink or blue on the top.

Wedding Anniversaries
Not everyone celebrates wedding anniversaries, but some are considered special and may prompt a party—the twelve-and-a-half-years', twenty-fifth, and fiftieth particularly. Sometimes you will be asked by a family member to contribute to a special book that is being compiled for the couple, with stories, for example, from their actual wedding day. There is often also a *Ceremoniemeester* to dispense advice. You will probably be asked to join in singing a song that has been specially composed by friends or family for the couple. A sheet of words is provided—if you can't read or understand them, just hum the chorus!

Retirement Parties
These are sometimes provided by the organization from which the person is retiring. The retiree is allowed to invite a number of people from work and home for coffee and cake or a buffet—how elaborate depends on the organization. A collection is made at work for a gift (see also pages 88 and 149) and people coming from outside the company bring their own

present. It is more important to choose something that reflects the interests of the recipient than to buy an expensive present. If a work party is not arranged the family may organize one instead.

HISTORICAL OCCASIONS

Some national events have an historical origin or context. The main ones are listed below.

May 4: Remembrance Day (Dodenherdenking). The official commemoration day for all the people killed in military conflicts or in peace-keeping situations since the outbreak of the Second World War. Flags are hung at half-mast outside people's houses and memorial services are held. At 8:00 p.m. there is a two-minute silence, which the vast majority of the population respects, in remembrance of the dead.

May 5: Liberation Day (Bevrijdingsdag). This celebrates the liberation of the Netherlands by the Allied Forces in 1945. Flags are hung outside houses.

June–August: Local festivals and fairs are held in many towns nationwide. These are often celebrations of historical events or folk traditions, and give a special insight into the history and customs of the different parts of the Netherlands.

September: State Opening of Parliament (Prinsjesdag). On the third Tuesday in September, the King rides to Parliament in The Hague in a golden coach through streets lined with cheering people. He reads the Speech from the Throne (*Tronrede*) setting out the government's policy for the year ahead.

chapter four

MAKING FRIENDS

The Dutch are very sociable—with family, friends, and in the local community. Living closely together is very much part of Dutch life (literally, in urban areas), and they spend time building up relationships in order to maintain harmony in the *samenleving* (society). As a result, they are generally at ease in social situations, good at making conversation, and relaxed in their manner. They are usually interested in other people and keen to make visitors feel welcome and comfortable, but there are a couple of exceptions to this. In the cities, people may simply be too busy to spare much time for making new friends. And in very rural areas you may find people more reluctant to make contact with strangers, although once the initial barriers have been overcome the Dutch instinct for hospitality will normally assert itself.

The Dutch are taught the value of social interaction from an early age, when they are expected to make an effort to attend social events and join in. This carries on into adult life, and a Dutch family ends up with rather a lot of commitments—family events, regular contact with friends, activities at clubs or societies, and often involvement with the local community. Certain conventions keep this busy social life under control and running smoothly. The Dutch tend to make appointments rather than visit spontaneously, and it is generally understood how long certain types of visit will last.

ATTITUDES TOWARD FOREIGNERS

Dutch people are generally friendly toward foreigners and will help out if you ask for assistance. If you want to talk to somebody, it is appreciated if you try to speak a bit of Dutch, although your attempts may well be met with a smile. "*Spreekt u Engels alstublieft?*" is the polite way to ask if someone speaks English. Normally, at the sound of an American or British accent, the person will switch immediately to English to reply. The Dutch are good at languages and they are usually delighted to speak to you in English.

The majority of the population does not tolerate racist attitudes, and people are generally pleasant.

The vote for Brexit and the election of Donald Trump has altered the attitude of some toward Britain and America, but politeness and hospitality are so ingrained in Dutch behavior that you are unlikely to notice. People can also be keen to comment upon or to ask you about the politics in your own country, so be prepared!

If you are staying in the Netherlands for a while, you may well find yourself invited to someone's home. Many Dutch people are curious about visitors from abroad and take the opportunity to find out more about them by being sociable. Remember, however, that they are sometimes too tied up with family and old friends to have much time over for new ones. If you feel you have "clicked" with somebody and want to take the friendship further, take the initiative and persevere, but if a suggestion to get together is declined more than twice, you would be wise to back off.

There is a saying in the Netherlands: "*De kat uit de boom kijken.*" This translates as "The cat looks on from the safety of the tree," meaning "Being curious but wary!" Some people are interested in foreigners but a bit unsure about getting involved with them, possibly because they are not confident about speaking other languages or perhaps because they do not have the time and energy to invest in it. If you want to meet them, it will be up to you to learn some basic Dutch and to make the first move. A normal coffee morning, Dutch style, is a safe start. Have some "props" on hand—a few photos or pictures of your hometown or country perhaps—to help the conversation along, and keep it fairly short until the relationship gets on a more relaxed footing.

HOW TO MEET THE DUTCH

It is easy to meet people if you are prepared to be proactive and not to wait for others to come to you. It is possible to make friends with colleagues and meet on a social basis. Also, many Dutch people join a sports club or activity group. This is an ideal

way to meet people with similar interests. It is also easier to communicate with people who are not very confident in their spoken English if you are doing something practical.

The important thing about making contact with Dutch people is to be prepared to put some effort into it and to persevere. The onus is on you to convince them of the value of your friendship. This can take a while, but once it has been achieved you will have made loyal friends who will stick with you. In the meantime, enjoy the opportunity to meet all kinds of different people until you find those individuals you would like to know better. If you move into a house or apartment, introduce yourself to the neighbors and invite them over for coffee or an evening drink.

If you say that you would like to meet up with somebody in the future, you have to mean it when you say it, and, most importantly, follow it up. Otherwise, you will be seen as shallow, and will be given the cold shoulder at your next meeting. Be direct—do not say "yes" to a Dutch person if you only mean "maybe," and don't say "maybe" if you already know that the answer is "no!" They will just find your prevarication irritating and rude.

VRIENDEN OF KENNISSEN? (FRIENDS OR ACQUAINTANCES?)

Do not assume friendship with Dutch people too quickly. However well you seem to be getting on, they may regard you only as an acquaintance. Don't take this personally. In the same way that the Dutch have two levels of family, they have two levels of friendship. The close family is known as *het gezin*—mother, father, brothers, sisters, and perhaps grandparents. Then there is *de familie*—members of the extended family (aunts, uncles, cousins, and so on). The two levels of friendship are *vrienden*— people they have known for a long time, who have supported their Dutch friend (and have been supported in return) through sad as well as happy times—and *kennissen*—people whom they may regard with affection, but see only occasionally and do not know intimately. *Vrienden* are considered as *trouw*—loyal and reliable. It takes time and effort to be accepted into the close circle of a Dutch person or family and referred to as a *vriend*. If you are referred to as a *kennis* this does not mean that you are disliked or not accepted; it just means that you haven't quite earned your dues yet.

GREETINGS

Greetings in the Netherlands are fairly formal. When introducing yourself, in either a social or a business situation, you should shake hands firmly, smile, look the other person straight in the eye, and tell them your full name, as in "Good morning. Thomas Parkinson." If they use their first name in their greeting, it usually indicates that you can use it when addressing them, but when speaking to people older than yourself use their surname, until they invite you to use their first name. When you leave a social event, you are also expected to shake hands before you go. If there are a lot of people present, you can get away with a general good-bye and wave to the group as a whole, but make sure you shake hands with your hosts. If you are friendly with them, you can give them three light kisses on alternate cheeks, continental style. Men, however, do not generally kiss each other—a firm handshake is fine!

You will find that children are also expected to "give their hand." When arriving at a social event, even very young children are encouraged to go around the group of guests shaking hands and saying a formal "hello." When they leave, they are expected to offer their hand to the hostess to say "thank you" and "good-bye."

JOINING CLUBS, SOCIETIES, AND CLASSES

Clubs and societies are very popular in the
Netherlands, and they exist for all sorts of activities.
Joining one is an excellent way of meeting Dutch
people who share your interests. To find out what is
available, look online, go to the local library, or ask
at the *stadhuis* (town hall).

Another good way to make friends is to go to
Dutch language classes. Learning even a few phrases
will help to smooth the way, and Dutch friends and
acquaintances will greatly appreciate the fact that
you are trying to fit in. Local *Volksuniversiteiten*
offer adult education classes. See https://www.
volksuniversiteit.nl/information-in-english for
more information. Further education colleges also
run courses; these are more expensive but are run
to standards set by the government. Check on the
Internet for local college details.

EXPAT INFO
The larger cities also have various expatriate clubs that may provide some good ways of meeting people—check with your embassy, or have a look at the listings given in the following publications:

ACCESS Magazine
ACCESS is a nonprofit organization with offices in The Hague and Amsterdam. It provides information to English-speaking people living in the Netherlands on a range of topics, including club/society contact information.

The NL Times
This is a nationally distributed paper containing items relevant to the expat community in the Netherlands.

www.expatica.com
A Web site with excellent information on all aspects of living in the Netherlands, including club/society listings.

www.angloinformation.com and www.iamsterdam.com
Web sites with listings of English-language media available in the Netherlands.

GASTVRIJHEID (HOSPITALITY)
The Dutch go to great lengths to make visitors feel welcome. If you are on their territory—be it in a house, office, or store—as a guest, they see it as their responsibility to make the situation as *gezellig* as

possible. If you visit an office on a regular basis you are likely to be treated as a colleague after your first few visits.

Invitations Home
If you are invited to a Dutch person's home you should accept if at all possible. If you turn down an invitation it may not be repeated, unless your reason was particularly convincing.

You will find that everything is ready for your arrival, and that care has been taken to create a pleasant and welcoming atmosphere. Don't arrive early—this is considered impolite. Arriving more than ten minutes or so late is also frowned upon. And don't expect to be given a tour of the house, as happens in some other countries; this is not a normal part of a visit.

Never "drop in" for a visit unannounced. The less you know a person, the more notice you need to give. If you have a good relationship with somebody, you could phone in the morning to see if it would be acceptable to pop in later in the day.

ENTERTAINING
There are certain conventions for entertaining that you should know about. For people at home during the day, morning coffee is an opportunity to catch up with friends' or neighbors' news and views. You may be invited to join Dutch friends for morning coffee on the weekend. Strong, freshly brewed coffee will be served (instant coffee is regarded as a poor substitute). "*Koffiemelk*" (a sweet condensed milk) or warm frothy milk will

be on offer, and there will be cookies or a piece of cake. Do not take anything until it has been offered to you, as this will be considered bad manners. Even if you have been casually invited to help yourself, take only one biscuit or slice of cake until you are offered again—you are not expected to pig out!

If you are invited to dinner, it will probably start fairly early—generally 6:30 or 7:00 p.m.—and you will be expected to be on time. If a toast is proposed during the meal, the correct word to use is "*proost*" (pronounced to rhyme with "toast") when raising your glass to the people present. After the meal, there will be some more conversation, but do not outstay your welcome—you are unlikely to be allowed to help with the tidying and washing up and your hosts will not want to get to bed too late. During the week, aim to leave between 10:30 and 11:00 p.m. On weekends you could stay longer.

If you are invited to come for a *borrel* (drink), at around 7:30 or 8:00 p.m., this will not be a proper meal. You will need to eat your evening meal before you go, but leave room for *borrelhapjes* (savory snacks). Upon arrival, you may well be offered

coffee and a piece of sweet tart to start, followed by a choice of alcoholic or soft drinks, normally with some *borrelhapjes*. Sticking to tea or coffee is considered rather *ongezellig*, so ask for a fruit juice or soft drink if you do not want alcohol.

GIFT GIVING
In the Netherlands it is normal to give gifts to people at work on their birthday or on a special occasion, such as a long-service celebration or retirement. Usually, these are given jointly by the team or department and a collection will be made to pay for them. It is not necessary to give a personal or individual present in these situations. Gifts may be given on behalf of the company to visitors from other countries.

Gift giving is also a part of social life. If you are invited home by Dutch friends and it is the first time that you have been to their house, or if you are going for a meal, it is usual to bring flowers, special chocolates, or a decent quality bottle of wine. If you are going for morning coffee it is not necessary to bring a gift (unless you are visiting for the first time), although some homemade cookies, typical of your country, will be appreciated. The Dutch do not want you to spend vast amounts on presents. They find this embarrassing and a waste of money, and do not want to feel obliged to do the same in return if they visit you.

THE DUTCH AT HOME

The Dutch are very family-orientated. At home they combine hard work—keeping it in good condition both outside and within—with a determination to make the most of any opportunities for relaxation and enjoyment.

QUALITY OF LIFE

The Netherlands is still relatively prosperous, and most Dutch people enjoy a good quality of life, although there are certainly poor families, particularly in the bigger cities. Life for the majority

is divided between work (paid or voluntary), time in the home or spent with company elsewhere, and enjoyment of the great outdoors. The economic situation picked up in 2014 and since then there has been a steady recovery, with the national unemployment rate decreasing and a gradual rise in house prices.

LIVING CONDITIONS

Apartments and houses in the Netherlands are small compared to those in America and Britain, and can seem rather cramped. However, the Dutch have a talent for making the best use of any space available to them. Staircases are narrow and steep so that they occupy as little space as possible. In most houses the attic (the *zolder*) is used as living space and typically comprises a bedroom or two and an area for dealing with laundry.

If you are living in an apartment complex, you will normally find that there are rules about the use of public areas. Before you sign a lease, be certain that you know what your obligations will be as a tenant. If you infringe the rules you will cause offense, and somebody will come to tell you that your behavior is out of order. You may also find that you are expected to take part in the maintenance of the communal areas—this is not always carried out by the caretaker or landlord.

SCHOON, NETJES, EN GEZELLIG (CLEAN, NEAT, AND COZY)

Neatness is important because space is at a premium and cannot be wasted under a layer of clutter. Children are encouraged to help in keeping the home looking clean and tidy. Perhaps surprisingly, the emphasis on cleanliness and neatness does not result in a cold and unwelcoming atmosphere. The Dutch are very skilled at creating a *gezellig* atmosphere in the home.

FURNISHINGS

If you are staying for a while and decide to rent, it is advisable to get assistance from a real estate broker (*makelaar*). The laws involved and the manner of concluding a contract are complicated and so different from America and Britain that it is worth hiring a professional to act on your behalf. The best way to choose an agent is to ask expatriate acquaintances to recommend someone who has provided a good service for a decent price. Reputable real estate agents are members of the Netherlands Estate Agents Foundation (Nederlandse Vereniging van Makelaars, or NVM).

There are a few things that you need to be aware of. More than 40 percent of Dutch people rent their homes. Competition for private rentals is fierce so be prepared to look in a wide area and to sign quickly when you find a property that you like.

The description of an apartment or house as "unfurnished" ("*kaal*") means precisely that. There will be nothing in the apartment at all: no light fittings, floor coverings, or appliances, although there will be a basic kitchen and bathroom without white goods. A semi-furnished property ("*gestoffeerd*") means that there may be floor coverings, curtains, and some basic appliances, but make sure that you know precisely what is included.

A furnished property ("*gemeubileerd*") will usually have nearly everything that you need to be able to move in and function normally—china, cutlery, kitchen appliances, lights, and the like. However, do not take for granted items such as a dishwasher, television, DVD player, radio, bedding, or even an oven.

The Dutch do not have room in their apartments and houses for huge refrigerators, washing machines, and freezers, so appliances tend to be small, especially in comparison to those in American homes. Washing machines are connected to the cold water supply only. Many visitors buy new appliances in the Netherlands and sell them to other expatriates when they leave.

When renting a property, you will usually be required to pay the first month's rent in advance, plus a deposit of an extra month or two. Make sure that you know which utilities are included in the rent as this can vary. For those that are your responsibility, arrange for the bills to be sent directly to you so that you can deal with them quickly and efficiently. Be clear about any shared costs, such as a contribution to the upkeep of communal areas. Make a detailed inventory before you move in, listing everything in the property and identifying any problems; otherwise you may end up being charged for repairs to something that was broken before your arrival.

Dutch rental laws generally favor the tenant. If you engage a *makelaar* to act on your behalf, they will be aware of your rights and will explain them to you. Do not discuss the rental agreement with your landlord without your *makelaar* present. Verbal agreements are legally binding, and there are unscrupulous landlords, as there are anywhere, who may take advantage of your lack of knowledge. Read the fine print, and if you are at all unsure ask for expert advice before signing anything.

The following Web sites have useful information on how to go about renting accommodation and have links to property portals in English:

• www.expatica.com
• www.iamexpat.nl
• www.expatfocus.com
• www.iamsterdam.com

APPLIANCES

Dutch plugs are two-pronged and use 220 volts and 50 hertz. If you are American, it is not worth bringing electrical equipment with you as you will need to use transformers. British equipment can be used with normal adapters. American televisions cannot be used because they operate on a different system. American DVDs are incompatible with European players. Normal home computers require expensive transformers, but laptops are especially adapted to be able to operate in Europe. Generally, it makes far more sense to buy locally and to sell when you leave.

IDENTITY

The Dutch have a non-compulsory identity card scheme. Citizens over the age of fourteen are required to carry some form of identification at all times in case this is asked for by police or other official agents. Most people use the identity card for this, but driving licences or passports and other forms of identification can also be used. As a visitor you will also need to carry identification. If you are staying for less than three months, you do not need a visa to enter from America or from other European countries. All you need is a valid passport.

If you are intending to stay for longer than three months, you should contact the Justitie Immigratie-en Naturalisatiedienst (IND) to get more information about changing your status. The Internet homepage has an English version and there is a program allowing you to specify the nature of your planned stay and advising on what needs to be done, depending on your nationality. You may have to be registered on the Population Register (Bevolkingsregister) at the town hall before you register with the Aliens Police. Check with the information office at the town hall or police station if you are not sure where to go. To register for work you need to obtain a work permit (*werkvergunning*) unless you are an EU citizen. You also need to apply for a BSN (social service number—*burgerservicenummer*, previously called the Sofi or Social-Fiscal number), in order to pay tax and national insurance. British nationals will need to wait for the outcome of the Brexit negotiations to see where they stand on these matters, but until Brexit is finalized they are still EU citizens.

All registrations involve a lot of bureaucracy and you need to be patient. However, if you do not register life will become impossible because you cannot function in Dutch society without the necessary documentation.

DAILY LIFE AND ROUTINES

The Dutch get up at about 6:30 to 7:30 a.m., and the family usually has breakfast together before going their separate ways to work and school. On weekends, people may stay in bed for a bit longer. If you stay in a Dutch home, you will please your hosts if you make an effort to fit in and adapt yourself to their routines. Ask what they normally do. Some Dutch families attend church on Sunday, and you can decide what you want to do instead if you do not want to join them.

Breakfast normally consists of bread with a choice of ham, cheese, boiled egg, jams, or other sweet toppings, and perhaps yogurt. There may be cereals. You will be offered tea, coffee, milk, or fruit juice. Most people set off for work between 7:00 and 8:00 a.m. Schools begin at 8:15 or 8:30 a.m.

Lunch is a light meal, with a simple cheese or meat sandwich and soup, or fried eggs, ham, and bread. To drink there is fruit juice, milk, water, tea, coffee, or beer. Most children (especially at primary school age) go home for lunch; some take a packed lunch to school.

When children come home, at around 3:30 p.m., they generally have a light snack. Many then take part in sporting or other extracurricular activities. Of course, the older ones, from about the age of nine, also have homework.

Early evening is the time for the main family meal, usually served around 6:00 p.m. This is the main meal of the day and it normally consists of meat, potatoes, and vegetables, although foreign foods such as pizza, pasta, rice dishes, or noodles are also popular. Do not telephone Dutch people at this time! It will be considered a nuisance. If visitors are invited, the evening meal may start a bit later. There are the same drinks as at lunchtime, although wine may also be offered. People generally go to bed between 10:30 and 11:00 p.m. during the week, and later on weekends.

ATTITUDES TOWARD CHILDREN

Children are encouraged to be social. They attend many organized activities, and often belong to sports

clubs or other youth groups. They play together after school in each other's houses, in designated play areas, or on the streets. If the playing gets rough, adults tend not to intervene unless they have to. It is up to the children to sort out disputes for themselves. "*Je moet leren om voor jezelf op te komen.*" ("You have to learn how to stand up for yourself.")

Some Dutch children can seem rather outspoken. They often address their parents by their first names from an early age, and their parents' attitude toward them can seem relaxed to outsiders. Generally the Dutch like their children to make their own choices about how they conduct their lives. However, they do lead by example and ensure that their children are very clear on what their values are and about what is expected of them. In this way, gentle pressure is exerted to conform— it is not turned into a confrontation.

SCHOOLS AND SCHOOLING

Education is free up to the age of sixteen (after that there is a minimal contribution), and Dutch schools are funded by the state, even though many of them are private or religious. We have seen that for years social and religious harmony was maintained in the Netherlands by the system of "pillarization." Groups from different sections of the community educated their children separately. Even today this is evident—Catholic, Protestant, Liberal (nondenominational), Socialist, Jewish, Islamic, and Hindu schools all exist. They are all obliged to teach the same curriculum, but the emphasis on the values of the school and the way that the religious calendar is observed will vary.

Most Dutch children start the *basisschool* (elementary or primary school) at the age of four, although attendance is not compulsory until they are five years old. At the end of their primary education most children sit the *Cito-toets* (Cito-test) to determine (with parental input) which level of education might best suit them. Children attend secondary school from the age of twelve to sixteen, seventeen, or eighteen, depending upon which direction they want to take for their future studies and eventual employment. The different types of education are often provided in the same building so that it is possible to transfer from one to another if the need arises. The exceptions to this are the *gymnasia*, which cater only to the most academic children. If a child attending a *gymnasium* consistently fails to make the grade, they will have to move schools.

All children at secondary schools take the same subjects for the first one to two years (the *brugklas*—"bridge class") and within that time it will be decided which type of education they will follow. Children who are more suited to practical work can attend VMBO pre-vocational education (available at four different levels), which lasts for four years and gives them a basic secondary education and the chance to learn practical skills. Then they have to attend further education classes related to their chosen field of work for a number of days per week until the age of eighteen. The HAVO stream prepares children to enter higher professional education and enables them to leave school at seventeen. Once they have finished the school program, their employer is required to send them to college for so many days each week to complete work-related qualifications until they are eighteen. The VWO stream prepares the children to enter university, although they may choose to enroll in higher professional education courses instead. Children are regularly assessed in school and if their grade average increases or decreases significantly they can be moved between the different levels of education.

Children who have learning difficulties or other special needs can attend schools that cater specifically to their needs and that are designed to enable them to reach their potential in a caring environment.

There are now also many TTO (*tweetalig onderwijs*—bilingual) schools available. These schools teach some of the subjects on their curriculum solely in the English language and the rest of the curriculum in Dutch. There are also many international schools—either nationality based, or where the subjects are taught entirely in English.

Public Knowledge

When young people have passed their diploma examinations—whether at sixteen, seventeen, or eighteen—their parents will have a family celebration or treat them to a party. If they have been successful, a school bag will be hung on the flagpole outside the house for the whole community to see. This can seem a bit harsh for children who haven't passed, but if the bag is not there people know to commiserate and give encouragement for the future.

There are fourteen Dutch research universities and many universities of applied sciences, plus colleges of higher education. These are financed by the state, but higher education is not free and students (or their parents) have to contribute. Many young people live at home while studying at university or higher education colleges because accommodation is scarce and costs are high.

The Dutch system is now more in line with the American and British systems, and students can work towards a bachelor's degree, a master's degree (giving the title *doctorandus*—"Drs" is often seen on Dutch business cards)—or for some to go on to attain their Ph.D. Graduating from university is another special occasion for Dutch students and is celebrated by the family, as well as with friends.

RESOLVING COMPLAINTS
In the Netherlands complaints are normally resolved by talking things through. It is considered important to avoid outright confrontation when a friendly word will solve the problem. The main aim is to preserve harmony and to come to a mutually agreed solution. If anyone's behavior is causing a nuisance, the offender can expect someone from the community to come and discuss the matter with them. If the

matter cannot be resolved after it has been discussed on a one-to-one basis, it will be referred to the relevant authority to deal with—the local residents' association, a local government office, or the police. The Dutch use regulations to try to get a balance between preserving the individual's right to freedom of expression and lifestyle, and the needs of the community as a whole.

CHANGING LIFESTYLES

Many outsiders perceive the Netherlands to be an increasingly permissive society, as it is often at the forefront of legal reform. Legalized prostitution, homosexual rights, the decriminalization of soft drugs, and legalized euthanasia are controversial matters that have stimulated great debate. However, these changes to the law do not affect the lives of the vast majority of Dutch people.

The greatest changes to the Dutch way of life have been caused by new technology and globalization. Technology has stimulated consumerism, and globalization has reduced the differences between the Netherlands and other countries.

Some areas of the country still adhere to strict religious beliefs and a very conservative way of life; others are home to people living alternative lifestyles. For the majority of the population, however, conformity is the order of the day, and keeping to the general norms and values in order to promote a peaceful society (*samenleving*) is still an essential part of the Dutch way of life.

chapter six

TIME OUT

The Dutch work from 36 to 40 hours a week, and have four or five weeks' vacation allowance a year. Overtime is not usual, and there is little pressure to stay at work beyond the normal contracted hours, although managers may be required to work unpaid overtime. Those restricted to school vacations tend to travel in Europe or stay in the Netherlands—they may rent a house in the country, or go sailing on the lakes or around the waterways. Some people accumulate extra days to enable them to take the occasional long vacation, but this depends on their contracts.

The Dutch are very fit and active outdoors. There are marked routes and opportunities to go walking, jogging, cycling, roller-skating, or roller-blading.

Ask at the tourist information center (the Vereniging voor Vreemdelingenverkeer, or VVV) or at an ANWB (motoring association) shop for booklets with the routes for your area. There are often designated picnic areas along the way, or you can take a break at one of the many cafés.

SHOPPING

Shops in the Netherlands are called *winkels*, pronounced "vinkels." To shop is *winkelen*, which means browsing around clothes shops and the like, or *boodschappen*, which means to shop for necessities. Most shop assistants in the larger central stores speak English.

The Dutch do their *boodschappen* quickly and efficiently in local shops or supermarkets. They enjoy cooking with fresh ingredients, and tend to shop every other day for fresh produce and once or twice a week for general items. The joy of food shopping in the Netherlands is the abundance of specialty shops, usually of excellent quality. Some sell *biologische* (organically produced) food, which is more expensive. If you go into a small shop, you should wish the shop assistant and the other customers a "Good day" (see page 155). The staff in smaller shops may not speak English but are usually happy to work out what you want.

The *bakkerij* (bakery) sells fresh bread and rolls, pastries, cookies, cakes, and sometimes homemade chocolates. The *slagerij* (butcher) sells fresh and cooked meat and some sausages. The *visverkoper* (fishmonger) sells fresh fish and some cooked fish to eat as a finger-food snack (not like British fish

and chips). The *groenteboer* (greengrocer) sells fresh fruit and vegetables. A *kruidenwinkel* (herb shop) has herbal teas and other drinks, remedies, toiletries, and natural foodstuffs. A *drogisterij* (chemist) sells general products such as over-the-counter medicines (often including homeopathic remedies), hygiene products, and cosmetics. The *apotheek* (pharmacy) is a separate shop for the sale of medicines and the dispensing of prescriptions. Pharmacies have weekend hours to ensure that prescriptions can be collected in an emergency.

Many towns have at least one weekly market (*markt*) where you can buy a variety of goods for a set price—no haggling. Some larger towns have a separate flower market each week. Every so often there is also a *rommelmarkt* (flea market), where members of the public as well as traders can hire a stall and sell secondhand or cheap goods. Here you can try to get the price down—it's an accepted part of the fun. Find out the date, time, and place of any markets at the VVV, the town hall information

office, or by checking the local newspapers. Better still, ask a Dutch neighbor or friend.

When out shopping, be prepared to hold your own, or you run the risk of being jostled out of the way and ignored. Some shops (including post offices and banks) have a ticket dispenser, so that your ticket number determines the order in which you are served. If there isn't a ticket system, lines tend to be rather loosely formed and can come from two directions at once. Or there is a huddle, and the shop assistant will ask, "*Wie is nu aan de beurt*?" ("Whose turn is it next?") When it is your turn, stick up for yourself politely and firmly, or you will still be standing there half an hour later. This fits in with the Dutch view that everybody has to stand up for their own rights and not depend on others to do it for them.

Shopping Times

Shops are generally open from 9:00 a.m. and close between 5:00 and 6:00 p.m. Most do not open until 12:00 noon or 1:00 p.m. on Monday to allow for shelf stocking or for staff training. There are exceptions: some bigger stores, supermarkets, and garden centers open on Monday morning. Once a week, usually Thursday or Friday, there is *koopavond* (evening shopping). Check this locally. On *koopavond* small shops may close for an hour's meal break at about 5:30 or 6:00 p.m., then open up again. *Avondwinkels* (convenience stores) are open until 1:00 a.m.

The main supermarkets stay open on weekdays and Saturdays until around 8:00 p.m. and may be open on Sundays but only for limited hours (check for details locally). Some gas stations are open twenty-four hours, but usually only in large towns or on the main highways. Shops and garden centers are allowed to open by law for a limited number of Sundays each year. Check in the local press—the Sunday openings are well advertised. Just before Christmas the shops are allowed to stay open for longer hours. In central Amsterdam the shops stay open for seven days a week until 10:00 p.m., and in tourist areas shopping hours tend to be longer.

Flowers
Flowers are cheap to buy and are beautifully arranged and presented in the shops. No town is without a large number of florists. Selling tulip bulbs is big business, and the Dutch also export a significant volume of cut flowers. The horticultural industry holds a national exhibition called the Floriade every ten years in a different area of the Netherlands. This is open to the public and is a great attraction for anybody who

is interested in flowers and plants. The displays at Keukenhof, the "Garden of Europe," show a wealth of spring flowers, including, of course, tulips.

A Dutch Icon

Apart from the thousands of brightly colored clogs for sale in all the tourist shops, wooden clogs are still regarded as useful for certain activities. They are sturdy, and keep the feet clear of mud, and are most likely nowadays to be found on farms, or on sale in local garden centers.

Mind Your Purse!

As is the case in other large cities in Europe, foreigners are seen as easy game by petty criminals. Keep your wits about you and be wary of anybody who approaches you in the street and tries to engage you in conversation, perhaps asking to borrow a cell phone, or asking for money. It is best to reply with a firm but pleasant "No, sorry," and to walk on, ignoring any further requests. Generally such people do not make a continued nuisance of themselves after they have been firmly but politely rebuffed.

BANKS

Banks are open on Monday to Friday from 9:00 a.m. to 5:00 or 6:00p.m. Only main banks are open on Saturdays and then for restricted hours—check details locally. You will find ATMs, called *geldautomaten*, outside nearly all banks. They usually accept Maestro, Cirrus, Eurocard, Mastercard, Visa, American Express, and Plus Systems.

The Netherlands is part of the Eurozone and the euro replaced the Dutch guilder in 2002. You can open an account with any of the main banks—for example the Rabo, SNS, ABN AMRO, or ING bank—or with the Postbank in the Post Office. The Dutch pay for purchases in shops either with cash (*contant*), with a "PIN" code debit card, or by contactless systems. Credit cards can be used for larger purchases but are not accepted in all shops, so ask first.

Bills are usually paid from the checking account (*rekening courant*). Standing instructions (*automatische overschrijvingen*) can be arranged for regular payments such as rent and club subscriptions, and direct debits (*machtigingen voor automatische overschrijvingen*) can be set up for gas, electricity, etc. If somebody comes to your home to provide a delivery, repair, or cleaning service they usually expect to be paid in cash, so make sure that you have enough on hand. They will also expect to be offered a cup of coffee! People working for you over a period of time—

for example, builders—will present you with a bill with their account number and ask for the money to be transferred into their account. This is done with an *overschrijvingsformulier*, a transfer slip. Internet banking is also popular in the Netherlands and will enable you to make transfers easily, especially if you set up a Dutch bank account. See www.expatica. com/nl for guidance on the practicalities.

Currency can be changed in large hotels, and at banks, post offices, *bureaux de change*, and at GWK (*Grenswisselkantoren*, literally "border exchange offices"). The official exchange rates at the GWK are often the best, and these offices can be found in most medium-sized and large railway stations.

EATING OUT

Interest in other cultures and the multicultural nature of the Netherlands is reflected in the wonderful choice of food. Most large towns have restaurants offering cuisine from all over the world at different levels of price and sophistication. Generally, the Dutch dress casually when going out for a meal, unless it is for a special occasion at an expensive restaurant. The menu is displayed outside, so you can gauge the price and choice before you go in. Most of the larger restaurants have at least one menu in English.

There are also restaurants that double up as cafés (*eetcafés*) serving Dutch-style food. These are usually clean, reasonably priced, simple and pleasant, with good fresh food and friendly service. They often start the day as a café, serving coffee and apple tart (*appelgebak*) in the morning, and then offer a simple

menu for lunch—
sandwiches, soup,
uitsmijter (fried eggs,
ham, and cheese served
on bread), salads, and
hot or cold drinks. Later
in the afternoon (from
about 5:00 or 5:30 p.m.)
the menu changes, and
it is possible to get a
cooked meal of good-
quality fresh produce
with a decent choice of

local or regional dishes. Dutch food is generally fairly
plain—meat, chicken, or fish with fresh vegetables.
Soups (try *erwtensoep*, pea soup) and hearty stews are
popular. Note that many small cafés and restaurants
are closed on Mondays, except on bank holidays.

Warning
Don't go into a "coffee shop" and expect coffee and
Dutch apple tart. Under the Dutch soft drugs policy,
"coffee shops" can sell customers up to five grams of
cannabis for personal use. Unless that is what you are
looking for, go to a café, a snack bar, or a department
store restaurant instead. Be aware that some of
the southern provinces of the Netherlands have
introduced a sales ban on cannabis to non-residents.

If you want a snack rather than a meal, there are
many options. Snack bars serve food that is quick
and easy to eat, and often have high tables that you

stand at. The idea is to eat and move on quickly. Such places normally sell *patat* or *friet* (fries, or chips), which you will be offered with *frietsaus* (mayonnaise) or *pindasaus* (spicy Indonesian peanut sauce). If you want ketchup, you will probably have to ask for it. You can also get *kroketten*, a soft meat-based filling, covered in breadcrumbs and fried, which is eaten dipped in mustard. They are extremely hot inside, so treat them with caution!

Bitterballen are similar in taste but shaped differently; *nasiballen* are fried rice balls; and *loempias* are Chinese fried spring rolls. If you are feeling brave, a typical Dutch dish is raw herring, which you hold by the tail, dip in diced raw onion, dangle over your mouth and bite. A real Dutch experience! Another special snack that you may come across being made on stands in the street, often at festivals or fairs, is *poffertjes*. These are mini-pancakes (silver-dollar pancakes), which are made on a hot griddle while you watch. You could also visit one of the many

Indonesian or Chinese restaurants where you can sit down to a meal, or collect a meal from the takeout (*afhaalcentrum*).

A good choice for a cheap Dutch meal in a relaxed environment is a visit to a *pannekoekhuis*, where you can buy pancakes (*pannekoeken*) with an amazing choice of fillings, savory and sweet. These are usually in holiday areas—often in the countryside—and they are a big hit with children.

Toilets
Toilets in a restaurant or café are usually free for customers. If you just pop in because you are desperate, you may have to pay—ask at the bar. Most department stores have toilets near the restaurant or café. These cost a few cents, which you give to the attendant on the way in, or leave in a dish on the way out. By the way, if you go to the toilet in somebody's house when visiting, be sure to leave it as clean and tidy as you found it.

DRINK
The main drinks consumed by the Dutch are coffee, beer, and wine. The Dutch favor strong, filtered coffee, and drink a vast amount of it. They are also known for their beer: Heineken is a Dutch brew, a large amount

of which is exported to America. Dutch beers vary in taste and strength. There are *wit bier* (blonde beers, which are cloudy), lagers, strong dark beers, fruit flavored beers, and seasonal beers, plus imported beers from other countries. A wide range of wines from all over the world can be bought in local supermarkets and wine merchants. The Dutch sometimes drink wine with their evening meal, at festive occasions, or just to relax and unwind in the evening.

You can try traditional Dutch alcoholic drinks such as *jenever* (Dutch gin, also spelled *genever*), and *advocaat* (eggnog). *Jenever* was originally used for medicinal purposes. Now it is drunk ice-cold from a shot glass filled to the brim, sometimes with a chaser of lager. Ladies usually drink *advocaat*, for example at a birthday party, after the coffee has been cleared away. It is made from brandy, egg yolks, and other ingredients and is very sweet. It is served in a liqueur glass, but people eat it from the glass using a small spoon rather than drink it. It is popular with the older generation.

Proost! (as we've seen, pronounced "proast") means "Cheers!" in Dutch. Dutch people enjoy drinking, but do so in moderation, and you are not expected to become drunk, objectionable, and *ongezellig* (unpleasant, unruly, and antisocial). Light snacks (*borrelhapjes*) are normally served with drinks to soak up the alcohol and enable people to have a good time without becoming inebriated. The penalties for drinking and driving are severe, and people will not encourage you to drink when they know that you have to drive afterward.

The most popular nonalcoholic drinks are fruit juices, bottled water, iced tea, and milk. You might try a *koffie verkeerd*, which translates literally as "wrong coffee," because it tastes like a café latte and is considered far too milky by most Dutch people to be regarded as proper coffee.

RESTAURANT ETIQUETTE

When you go into a café you can usually sit where you want, although you will be expected to pick a table that is appropriate to your number. Since 2014 smoking has been banned in all cafés and restaurants—even at private functions and after closing time. In a more expensive restaurant, you should wait to be shown to a table. Once seated, you will be offered a drink from the menu, then left to choose your meal, which you can order when your drink arrives. When your food is brought, you will be wished "*Eet smakelijk!*"—"Enjoy your meal!" You can reply "*Bedankt*"—"Thank you." If a person who is also about to eat says "*Eet smakelijk!*" to you, reply "*Smakelijk eten!*" To call a waiter say "*Pardon, meneer*" (or "*ober*"), or a waitress ("*Pardon, juffrouw*" (or "*mevrouw*").

Eating with your fingers is generally frowned upon—you will even be given a knife and fork with a sandwich—and so is cutting up your food and then eating it with just a fork. When you have finished eating, put your knife and fork together on your plate (angled at 4:20 on the clock!).

The staff will usually ask you if you are enjoying your meal. If you are, you can say that it is "*Heel lekker!*"("Very tasty!") If you have a complaint, try to resolve it with the waitress or waiter before calling for the owner or manager. Be polite and pleasant. The Dutch do not respond well to raised voices, and are likely to become distant and uncooperative rather than helpful.

You may also see dogs in cafés and restaurants. This is quite normal and is not considered to be particularly unhygienic. As long as the dogs are well behaved, and they usually are, they are tolerated.

To ask for your bill, say "*Mag ik de rekening alstublieft?*" If you need a receipt to claim business expenses, you can ask for one—"*Mag ik de kassabon hebben?*" or "*Mag ik bewijs van betaling?*"

TIPPING

You do not need to tip in snack bars. In cafés most customers just round up the change. In restaurants you can give a tip for good service of 5 to 10 percent, unless it is already included in the bill. Check to see if there is a service charge as these are becoming more common. Many Dutch people do not tip at all unless the service is exceptional. Be aware that service in the Netherlands is more relaxed and generally slower than you may be used to and take that into account.

SEX IN THE CITY

Dutch attitudes to sex are supposedly liberal and relaxed—everybody knows about Amsterdam's red light district (Rossebuurt). Prostitution is legal in the Netherlands, which stems partially from pure pragmatism. The feeling is that prostitution is inevitable, so it must be properly regulated, primarily to protect both customers and prostitutes, but also to ensure that the associated income is taxed. If you want to visit Amsterdam's red light district, you will be safe—it has the highest police presence in the city. Just watch out for the usual pickpockets and go around in pairs or groups. Women are unlikely to be harassed, but it is probably better not to wander around the area at night. Do not try to take photographs of or film the prostitutes (or in any of the sex clubs) as this is strictly forbidden.

Amsterdam is also famous as the Gay Capital of Europe and is a great place for LGBT travelers and residents. There are many gay and lesbian bars, clubs, and restaurants, and the city is at the heart of Gay Pride week at the end of July and the beginning of August. The highlight is the Canal Parade, with street parties and decorated boats going along the canals from Amstel toward Prinsengracht (see page 71). Gay tourists flock to the city and the resident gay community is large. There is a Homomonument at the Westermarkt and next to that is the Pink Kiosk, which provides the LGBT community with information. The legal age of consent for homosexual sex has been the same as for heterosexuals since the 1970s, and since 1998 same-sex marriages have been legalized.

Although homosexuals are protected from discrimination by the law, attitudes toward them differ from place to place. While many university towns have a gay community, people in provincial towns may not be as accepting of overtly gay or lesbian behavior as they are in Amsterdam.

LEISURE

There are many leisure activities to choose from in the Netherlands, both indoors and out. You can find out about these at the VVV, the local tourist information office, which has leaflets and booklets on local activities and activities further afield. You can also pick up useful information in the ANWB (the motoring association) shop, at the town hall information office, or in the local press.

In addition to the main festivals, many towns also have their own festivals. These can be good fun and give an insight into the local culture. Ask at the VVV office for details, or check out the Netherlands Board of Tourism and Conventions Web site—www.holland.com. For children there are also local *kinderboerderij* (children's farms), theme parks, and many good zoos.

HIGH CULTURE

The Dutch love of cultural activity goes hand in hand with civic pride and their belief in access for all. This is reflected in the number of theaters and concert halls

around the country where classical music, opera, ballet, and plays are performed on a regular basis. The Royal Concertgebouw Orchestra and the Netherlands Philharmonic of Amsterdam are world renowned, as are the three main ballet companies—the Netherlands Dance Theater, Het Nationale Ballet, and the Scapino Ballet of Rotterdam. There is also the Netherlands Opera Foundation, which performs in the Muziektheater in Amsterdam. It is possible to book tickets for performances at the theaters and concert halls box offices, through the VVV, or through special reservation booking offices, or online.

Check local papers for information about what is on in your area or visit the VVV office for information. You can get a season ticket for many theaters and concert halls, entitling you to advance bookings and to some discounts. Recitals are also held in many churches on weekends, and tickets can be bought at the door on the day of the performance. There are also small art-house cinemas.

The Dutch set great store by their cultural heritage and their history, and all self-respecting towns have at least one museum. There are also permanent outdoor exhibitions, for example, the Openluchtmuseum (open air) in Arnhem, the Zaanse Schans windmill village, and part of the Zuiderzee Museum. Some of the places that are called *musea* (museums) are art galleries. You can buy a *Museumkaart* that is valid for a year and gives free access to over four hundred museums and galleries throughout the country, including many of the main ones. The investment will pay for itself after a few visits. There are so many wonderful places to see and things to do that you will be spoiled for choice.

POPULAR CULTURE
Many of the theaters catering to audiences who enjoy the "high arts" also cater to those who enjoy more popular entertainment. There are musicals, lighter

plays, comedies, reviews, and cabarets. Large towns
have a mainstream cinema, usually with several
screens inside. Around Christmas time, traveling
circuses perform in theaters or in big tents set up on
the outskirts of town. No section of the community is
neglected and there is entertainment for people of all
ages and tastes.

COUNTRYSIDE PURSUITS
The Dutch go to the countryside as often as they can.
Boating and sailing are common pastimes, and people
flock to the lakes and waterways for rowing, canoeing,
or speedboating events, or else they belong to sailing
clubs. You can go on a canal tour (*grachtenrondvaart*)
to see parts of the countryside and the towns from
a different perspective. Horseback riding is popular
and there are riding schools where you can arrange
treks. Look in the Yellow Pages (Gouden Gids) under
"*ruiterschool*" or "*manege*" for details.

There are twenty national parks in the Netherlands
that offer the chance to see the fauna and flora
of different types of natural habitat. See www.
natioanaalpark.nl/299/en for information in English.
Try a visit to the Brabantse Biesbosch Nature Reserve,
the Hoge Veluwe National Park, or the Sand Dunes of
Texel. All the parks have marked paths and a visitors'
center. The Hoge Veluwe National Park is also the
location of the Kröller-Müller Museum, which
houses a large collection of Van Gogh paintings. You
could also visit Keukenhof—the famous flower park.
It is open from late March to mid May, and again, for
the Zomerfest (summer festival), from mid August to
mid September.

The Dutch do not just use their bicycles for getting
around during the week. It is common to see families
cycling in the countryside on weekends, or cycling
clubs out in force to enjoy one of the *fietsroutes*
(cycling routes). Many people also go hiking or
walking in the countryside. If you decide to do the
same, make sure that you stick to the *Wandelterreinen*

(designated walking areas), because certain parts of the countryside are protected nature reserves. Check with the VVV office for specified routes, or have a look at the Dutch Railway (NS) Web site, http://www. ns.nl/en, as this provides information in English about ideas for day-trips. It also includes cycling and walking routes that start and end at railway stations.

SPORTS

The Dutch like to be healthy and exercise regularly. Many people (including children who do not have organized sport at school) are members of sports clubs. They enjoy participating in sport, rather than just watching it on television, and generally consider it to be worth the time and effort. They are recognized on the international sports scene for their prowess in soccer, speed skating, hockey, tennis, volleyball, and cycling. They also like fitness training, walking, swimming, sailing, horse riding, gymnastics,

and skating. There are clubs for baseball and softball, and auto racing is followed with enthusiasm.

One key winter sporting event that attracts a huge amount of attention and excitement is the Elfstedentocht (Eleven City Tour). This is a speed-skating event through Friesland that can only take place when the temperature is low enough for all the canals along the route to freeze to sufficient depth. When the conditions are right, there is great excitement. A limit is placed on the number of participants and the route is lined with enthusiastic spectators. Anybody who cannot get there tunes in to the event on television.

chapter seven

TRAVEL, HEALTH, & SAFETY

What strikes visitors first is the vast number of bicycles, ridden by people of all ages. This is the most popular form of transport in the Netherlands. The next most notable feature is the efficiency of the public transportation system.

CYCLING

Dutch people cycle everywhere, and use a car only for longer distances. Most people have a bicycle, which means that there are literally millions of them about. You will be amazed at how many people can fit on to one bicycle.

Children learn to cycle from an early age. They cycle to school with one of their parents when they are young, or in groups of students when they are nearing the end of elementary or primary school. It is not uncommon for secondary school pupils to cycle nearly ten miles (sixteen kilometers) to school and back each day, whatever the weather.

If you want to try cycling for yourself, this is the ideal place for it. You can rent a bicycle for the day at many railway stations or from the larger cycle shops, or buy a secondhand one very cheaply. Many of the

rented bikes are fairly basic and have back-pedaling brakes. If you are not used to cycling you could pose a danger to other people, who will assume that you can ride as well as they can. If you feel a bit unsure, practice cycling in a park before you take to the roads.

NOTES FOR CYCLISTS

- **Obey the rules of the road.**
  These apply to cyclists as much as to other forms of transportation. Cycle lanes have their own traffic lights and signs. Where there are cycle lanes, use them. You are not allowed to cycle on the sidewalk, which is a danger to pedestrians.

- **Lock up your bike.**
  Thousands of bikes are stolen, as it is a lucrative trade. Buy a secondhand one. It will attract less attention than a sparkling new one. Buy a good solid lock for it and never leave it unlocked, even for five minutes—fix it to something immovable. If you buy a valuable new bike, get it insured.

- **Keep dry.**
  Buy yourself a waterproof jacket and trousers, or a waterproof poncho, and be prepared to dress in layers. It rains a great deal in the Netherlands. Dutch people hold umbrellas up while cycling and use just one hand to steer but it is best not to try this!

- **Maintain the bike.**
  Make sure that the bike is in reasonable condition before you ride it and take a repair kit in case of emergency. You must have a functioning headlight, rear light, and bell.

- **Don't drink.**
  It is a criminal offense to ride a bike when you are over the limit for drinking (over 0.5 percent blood alcohol level).

WALKING

The Dutch are far more likely to cycle or use public transportation. However, as we have seen, walking is a popular way to keep fit and many people walk for pleasure, either around the towns or in the countryside. As in any country, hitchhiking is risky and is rarely done in the Netherlands.

For the more adventurous visitor, there are special organized hikes across the tidal mud flats (*wadlopen*, walking across the mud flats). These endurance activities take place between May and October in the north of the country. They are good fun if you are fit and healthy, and do not mind being covered in mud and soaked to the skin; however, it is *essential* to go in a group with an experienced, registered guide.

PUBLIC TRANSPORTATION

Public transportation is of a very high standard.
The Dutch are used to an excellent level of service
and rely on it. The Dutch railway system, called the
Nederlandse Spoorwegen (NS), offers a convenient
alternative to driving. It is only two hours by train
from Amsterdam to the northernmost part of
the country, and only two and a half hours to the
southernmost part. If you are in a hurry, check that
you are not getting onto a *stoptrein*, as these stop
at all the small stations and take far longer to get
between main towns and cities than the *sneltreinen*
(high-speed trains) or intercity trains do.

You pay for tickets by purchasing a smart card
called an OV-chipkaart, either from a ticket machine
or from the ticket booth. The OV-chipkaart works
either as an electronic purse, which one tops up,
or as a means of storing a travel product such as
a season ticket. There are three types: one type is

disposable and for
single use, another
is an "anonymous
OV-chipkaart,"
which you pay
a one-off fee for
and can then load
credit onto. This
can be used for
the trains, buses,
trams, and metros.
It is also possible
to order a personal
OV-chipkaart
online. You need

a minimum amount of credit on the card for traveling by train and less for traveling by bus, tram, or metro. It is compulsory to check in and out before and after your journey and when changing operator or mode of transport; use the OV-chipkaart pillars to do this. The cards can be topped up at machines in supermarkets or tobacco shops.

Children under four can travel by train free but cannot occupy a seat. Children between the ages of four and eleven can get a very cheap "railrunner" fare when accompanied by an adult. There are many kinds of special discounted tickets. Have a look on the NS Web site to see what these are—www.ns.nl/en.

If you take a pet with you on the train you will be charged according to its size and the distance of the journey. You can also take your bicycle on the train. A fold-up bike can be taken free, as long as you have actually folded it. Normal bikes have to be paid for. Ask at the ticket booth. Other useful extra information on rail travel can be found at: www.amsterdamtips.com/tips/ns-netherlands-rail-network.php.

LOCAL TRANSPORTATION—BUSES, TRAMS, AND METROS

The buses usually link up with the railway timetable to provide an integrated transportation network. Buses perform a useful function for regional travel, and, along with the trams and metros, they provide transport in the cities and

towns. The buses run from 6:00 a.m. to 11:30 p.m.
You need to buy an OV-chipkaart for all forms of
public transportation—bus, tram, or metro. Be
aware that you cannot pay with cash on buses
and trams.

CAR AND DRIVER'S LICENSES

You have to be at least eighteen years old to drive in the Netherlands, and twenty-one years or over with at least a year's driving experience to rent a car. Tourists can drive in the Netherlands with a valid license from the United States or from Britain. You'll need to have held your license for longer than six months, and a normal license will need to be supplemented with an International Driver's License, which can be obtained from the Automobile Association.

The law in the Netherlands requires you to have third-party liability insurance. If you actually have comprehensive coverage, you must get proof of this from your insurer. This is known as a Green Card.

If you become a resident in the Netherlands and have a valid driving license that was issued in another country more than six months before your arrival, you can use it for up to 185 days (six months). You must ensure that you have either taken a test to acquire a Dutch license, or exchanged your own foreign license for a Dutch one within the six months.

If you do have to exchange your license it is not a quick process, so allow yourself at least four weeks. If you drive after the six months is up and still don't have a Dutch license you will be uninsured, which is illegal. You will also be uninsured while your application is being processed, so do not drive then either. This is a good time to try out the public transportation system!

The licensing requirements differ according to your country of origin, and there are some exceptions to the general rules. If you are in doubt about your own situation ask for advice at your country's embassy.

Parking

Many cities have park and ride services. There are plenty of multistory parking garages. Usually you take a ticket and pay at a machine on your way back to the car, either by cash, chip, or via cell phone. In blue zone areas you can park using a blue zone disc, which you can purchase at ANWB (car association) shops, tobacco shops, and police stations. There are also some parking meters.

The traffic police keep a sharp eye out for people who stay longer than allowed, and you will be fined if you do so. Occasionally in spring they come and leave a tulip tucked under your windshield wiper with a note to say that you have parked well—a bit of positive reinforcement!

Drinking and Driving

Drinking and driving is a criminal offense in the Netherlands. You can be fined heavily if you are over the 0.5 percent blood/alcohol level. This applies equally to driving a car or riding a motorbike, scooter, moped, or bicycle.

If your blood/alcohol level is over 1.8, your case will be taken to court and you may be banned from driving for a period of time as well as being fined.

ROAD SENSE IN THE NETHERLANDS

- Driving is on the right side of the road.
- Speed limits are 30 kmph (18.5 mph) in residential areas, 50 kmph (31 mph) in towns and cities, 80 kmph (50 mph) on secondary roads, 100 kmph (62 mph) on highways as they go through city areas, with a top speed limit of 120 kmph (74.5 mph) on expressways. Observe the limits.
- Speed cameras are being used increasingly to improve traffic control. If you are caught speeding, either you will be fined on the spot, or you will receive a bill in the mail. Pay promptly—the cost goes up the longer you leave it. If you have been speeding in an area where road repairs are being carried out, you can be fined up to 50 percent more than the normal rate for endangering the lives of the workmen.
- Familiarize yourself with the Dutch highway code and road signs.
- If you are on a road that is larger than the roads feeding on to it, you usually have the right of way. You will see marks like dragon's teeth across roads where traffic has to give way. At unmarked junctions or junctions between roads of equal size, traffic coming from the right has the right of way. If in doubt, slow down or stop, but look in your mirror first to ensure that a car is not going to run into the back of you.

- You are required by law to carry a warning triangle in case of accident and to use headlamp converters. It is recommended (but not compulsory) that you also have spare headlight bulbs, a first-aid kit, and a fire extinguisher in the car. You also need to have your car documents on hand in case you have an accident.
- In the event of a minor accident, you will need to exchange your car-rental details (if applicable), insurance details, and registration number, plus your name and address, with any other drivers involved. If somebody is injured in a car accident, you are legally required to notify the police. The emergency number is 112.
- Be *extremely* careful of cyclists. They do not always obey the rules of the road, but if you hit them, you are liable for damages. Give them plenty of space and be prepared for the unexpected. Watch out for people coming along cycling lanes.
- Roundabouts (traffic circles) can be dangerous because many people seem unsure of the right of way. If there are dragon-teeth markings on the roads feeding into the circle, then traffic already on it has the right of way. Not everyone realizes this, so be cautious. If there are *no* teeth markings, then you have to give way to the traffic coming on to the roundabout from

the right at every road feeding on to it. Also, watch out for cyclists. The cyclists on the cycle tracks going around usually have the right of way. Even if they don't, they behave as if they do; it is better to go along with this than to kill or injure somebody.

- When turning right, be aware that there may be a cycle lane going past you on the inside.
- Late at night some traffic lights are switched over to flashing amber, rather than working through red, amber, and green. This is to stop you having to wait at the lights when there is no traffic about. Approach the junction cautiously and note from the teeth marks on the road whether or not you have the right of way. There is a greater risk at nighttime of people driving (or cycling) recklessly due to alcohol or drug abuse— give cyclists a wide berth.
- Seat belts are required for all passengers. Children under three must travel in the rear of the car in an appropriate safety seat. Children age three to twelve may travel in the front if they are in a special safety seat, but only if there is no room in the back. It is illegal to use a cell phone while driving unless it is hands-free.
- If you are in a city that has trams, be aware that they always have the right of way.
- If you are riding a motorbike or moped it is compulsory to wear a crash helmet.

TAXIS

You can pick up one at a taxi stand in most towns—they are usually positioned at stations, near to shops or to attractions. Taxis can also be hailed in the street in some of the main cities, but they cannot stop anywhere they like, so be prepared for one to pass you by. In most towns and cities it is necessary to order a cab by phone. Look up the number in the *Gouden Gids* (Yellow Pages) under "taxis" or in the local directory (*gemeentegids*).

Treintaxis (train taxis) are also available at many stations. You can buy a ticket for these if you are going to travel somewhere by train and know that you will need a taxi at the other end, or you can pay the driver directly. The advantage here is that they are cheaper because you share them with other customers. *Treintaxis* operate within a defined area around the station—the area is shown on the taxi stand. You press the button and ask for a taxi to be sent to pick you up. When it arrives, it will wait for ten minutes to see if there are any other passengers, then the driver will work out the quickest way to drop you all off at your different destinations. For the return journey, you need to phone for the taxi half an hour before you need to be picked up.

There are alternatives to the normal taxis—Uber Taxis for example can be hailed via an app on your smart phone. Amsterdam even has bike taxis if you want to try something different!

WHERE TO STAY

Accommodation is generally of a high standard. Whether you are staying in a city hotel or a simple *pension*, it will normally be clean and comfortable.

Hotels are rated on a one- to five-star basis, with five-star hotels as the top quality. The ratings are determined by the hotel's amenities rather

than its ambience, and correspond fairly well with the equivalent rating in America or Britain, although the Dutch hotels are often smaller. Hotel types range from chain business/leisure hotels, to boutique hotels, to family run businesses. Anything with a rating below one star is either a *pension* or a

guesthouse. It is also possible to stay at hostels—
there are certainly many of them in Amsterdam. If
you are interested in staying at a hostel check out
those available at https://www.stayokay.com/en.

The Dutch really enjoy camping and caravaning
and there are a large number of campsites that
are also rated on a one- to five-star basis for their
amenities and facilities. Some farms are also
licensed to have a camping area. It is also possible
to stay in self-catering *trekkershutten* (camping
huts), which are more pleasant than their name
indicates. These are for hikers and cyclists and
are likely to be near the coast, on the Waddenzee
Islands in the north, or in wooded areas.

Bed and breakfast establishments are less
common than in America or Britain. It is possible
to find them in resort areas, but in provincial towns
they are few and far between. Private homes can
register at the VVV tourist offices as available to
take guests but the standard of rooms is extremely
variable. You can also rent a room or apartment
via Airbnb, but check that the host is complying
with the law for the area. Amsterdam particularly
is clamping down on people flouting the rules. For
guidance, see www.iamsterdam.com/en/plan-your-
trip/where-to-stay.

Boat rental is another option for
accommodation when traveling around the
country. You can rent a moored houseboat, or it is
easy to arrange a boat rental for traveling around
the waterways. You do not need a *vaarbewijs*
(boating license) for pleasure boats under
15 meters (49 feet), and which cannot go faster

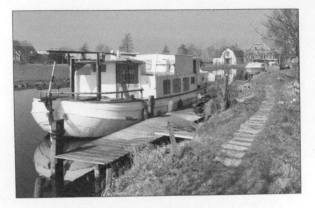

than 20 kmph (12.5 mph). The extensive network of waterways is easy to navigate once you have mastered the art of getting past the bridges and locks.

For more information on the great variety of accommodation available, go to a VVV tourist office or visit the ANWB (car association) shop. Both have books on sale that give full and up-to-date listings of different types of accommodation and their amenities. The VVV also has a booking service.

HEALTH

The Dutch health service is of a high standard. Members of the EU have a reciprocal health agreement entitling EU citizens to free medical advice and treatment. If you are British, take a European Union Health Insurance Card (EHIC) with you. You will have to pay for nonemergency treatment and then reclaim it later. If you are not an EU resident, be sure to take out travel insurance with medical coverage. If you decide to become a resident in the Netherlands you will need to purchase Dutch health care coverage—basic insurance cover

(*basisverzekering*) is compulsory. In case of emergency go to a hospital emergency department (*Eerste Hulp*) or to an emergency doctor's post (*Centrale Huisartsenpost*), or dial 112 for an ambulance. For more information contact your embassy; www expatica.com/nl also has useful information.

SAFETY

The Netherlands is generally safe, with very little serious crime. Take the usual commonsense precautions that you would anywhere, particularly to avoid theft. Some of these have been mentioned earlier (see pages 109–10).

chapter eight

BUSINESS BRIEFING

MAKING CONTACT

If you want to make business contacts, join professional associations and attend the meetings in your area, or go to courses or workshops, pop into business *beurs* (fairs) and talk to the people on the stands. Make sure that you always have good-quality business cards with you to hand out. Cold-calling is not acceptable. Ask someone to introduce you, or send an e-mail or letter to introduce yourself and the topic, and say when you will be getting in contact to make an appointment.

OFFICE STYLE AND ETIQUETTE

The Dutch business style is egalitarian. Nobody is seen to be more important than anybody else. Everybody has their part to play in the success of an organization, and this is acknowledged. Of course, people know who the boss is, and respect senior staff, but the respect is two-way and more dependent on the ability and motivation to do a good job than on hierarchical ranking.

Do not be deceived by appearances. People may dress casually and use first names with each other, but there is a focus on the business at hand. Surnames are used when dealing with unfamiliar business acquaintances—especially for people older than you—but you will normally quickly be invited to be on first name terms.

Working Practices

Quiet efficiency is a hallmark of successful Dutch business. Normal office hours in the Netherlands are generally from 8:00 a.m. to 5:30 p.m., Monday to Friday, with little or no office working on Saturday. Many people work flextime or part-time. Even some senior managers work part-time. Lunches are usually short and taken in the office or in the staff cafeteria with a quick sandwich and a drink.

Once rules have been agreed upon, discipline is self-imposed rather than imposed from outside. The Dutch are keen on punctuality. If you have an appointment, do not be late. It is unlikely that you will be able to reschedule an appointment at the last minute, as people plan their time carefully and well in advance. The office environment is clean, well-ordered, and quiet. The Dutch are noted for their good work–life balance—ranked third for this in the 2011 OECD table. They prefer to keep their time at home free for family and friends. You are unlikely to get a good reception if you disturb their evenings or weekend.

DUTCH BUSINESSPEOPLE

Dutch businesspeople enter the job market later than their British and American counterparts. As in Germany, there is a strong system of apprenticeship and on-the-job training. Key factors in promotion are education and qualifications, competence, hard work, ambition, and networking ability.

Today people working in all industries and organizations in the Netherlands have to be flexible. Contracts are often fixed-term, and it is not unusual

for employees to move on to another company within three to five years. Terms of employment are usually generous; however, it has been acknowledged that there is a gap between the rights of permanent and the increasingly diverse types of flexible workers. This has been addressed to a degree in recent legislation, but flexible workers are still disadvantaged. "Fringe benefits" such as company cars are rarely part of the basic employment contract. Bonuses are paid on some contracts, usually linked to performance reviews, but for the financial sector may not exceed 20 percent of annual pay.

Dutch egalitarianism and a sense of social responsibility mean that, in theory, women have equality in the workplace. In practice only about 20 percent of senior-level positions are filled by women. There is an increased level of financial independence for Dutch women and more now return to work after having children. Most women work part-time, often job-sharing.

COMMUNICATION STYLES

The Dutch tell you what they think, concisely and without frills. This can come across as abrupt, rude, or even arrogant to other nationalities. On the whole, exchanges are conducted with openness and without rancor. While the Dutch will tell you their views, they are also open to hearing your ideas. They expect professional people to be well informed and to have opinions on economic, business, and political matters. Be polite and friendly and do not get drawn into a discussion if you do not know what you are talking about: they will be unimpressed.

Foreigners sometimes mistakenly assume that the direct, relaxed, and egalitarian business culture of the Dutch implies an informal environment. The Dutch are in fact quite focused and expect the conventions of business to be adhered to. First-time contact is normally by e-mail, followed up by a phone call. When you are introduced to somebody, take your cue from them. If the person wants to be addressed by their professional title or surname, they will use it to introduce themselves. If they are formal, so should you be until invited to use first names.

There are standard conventions for business letters. The Dutch are particular about getting professional titles and forms of address correct when writing. If you are unsure about what title to use, find out before you send the letter. If you get it wrong, you could cause offense. When giving your own job title include your university degrees—higher education is valued in the Netherlands. Put only master's degrees and above. Common professional titles in the Netherlands are *Doctorandus* (drs) and *Ingenieur* (ir), both of which show that the person holds a masters-level degree.

Traditionally all verbal agreements used to be followed up in writing, but the pace of modern business does not always allow for this. However, an e-mail confirming the points agreed upon in a telephone conversation or in a meeting never goes amiss.

The Dutch like simple, clear information, and to get to the point quickly. Always give your name clearly at the start of a telephone conversation. Telephone conversations tend to be short and voicemails or texts are commonly used for messages, which are usually returned or acted upon quickly.

PRESENTATIONS

The Dutch expect detailed technical presentations, supported by relevant facts and data. A sincere approach is important: they distrust high-pressure, florid presentation styles. You should be well-informed, well-prepared, and to-the-point. Information should be presented in a positive manner, but without exaggeration. The Dutch will give you their full attention and make notes for future reference. You should do the same. They consider it important for the advantages and disadvantages of a new product, proposal, or service to be stated, and they expect to be given transcripts, brochures, and copies of any data presented. They look for price, quality, and delivery of service, and discussion of these must be included in a presentation. Make sure that you leave plenty of time for clarification of points.

Generally, businesspeople have a good grasp of English and can make themselves understood, even if their grammar and pronunciation may sometimes be a bit off the mark.

The Dutch expect to enter into direct and vigorous debate; outspoken questioning is a sign of interest rather than antagonism. Frankness and openness are the watchwords of discussion, and it is important that you express your views clearly. Any "beating around the bush" may be perceived as deviousness, and if you try to bluff, your bluff will be called. It is important not to speculate, and you will gain more respect for being open about limitations and constraints. If you mean "no," say "no," and do not give tentative answers. Don't make any promises that you can't keep.

The Dutch generally do not go in for small talk within business meetings. They will happily talk about more general matters over lunch or dinner, or perhaps over coffee before the meeting starts. The Dutch have a wry sense of humor, quite similar to British humor in some respects. Subjective feelings or emotions have no place in a business discussion, and are regarded as inimical to clear, rational, decision-making. Flowery language, flattery, and rhetoric are regarded as false and suspect.

Many Dutch people have a strong sense of social justice and social democracy, and may react adversely to extreme right-wing views. Be careful not to sound superior about your own or your country's achievements as they do not respond well to bragging, and do not criticize the Dutch, even if you seem to be being invited to do so.

TEAMWORK

If you are running a Dutch team, or working with one, what can you expect? In the Netherlands a team is a group of individuals united for greater efficiency and profit under a strong leader, chosen for specific technical competencies. To work well they each need a clear understanding of their responsibilities and authority.

Consultation is a key feature. Although the team leader's decision is final there must be consultation on all key issues and all team members are invited to give their views on the subject under discussion. This can take a great deal of time and outsiders can regard the process as irritatingly long. However, there is no rushing it along. The Dutch set great store on giving everybody the right to express their opinion and make a contribution. Once a decision has been reached, action will be taken and the necessary paperwork completed.

Dutch team members expect competence, reliability, and a rational approach to problem-solving from their leader. They appreciate sincerity, openness, and constructive criticism. They react badly to pretentiousness and flippancy. Do not treat them lightly, or ignore details.

GEZELLIGHEID AT WORK

The concept of *gezelligheid* extends into the work environment. If you are visiting a company in the Netherlands, you may well find that you are expected to join in with colleagues on social occasions such as birthdays or retirement parties. You may also be invited to participate in office outings. It is important to take part at least occasionally in order to cement bonds with your colleagues.

THE IMPORTANCE OF GOOD WORKING RELATIONSHIPS

Brian is a fairly reserved British manager. Whenever he visited the Netherlands for his work with a Dutch company, he was invited to join in the end of week *borrelje* (a quick drink). Being the quiet type, Brian far preferred a meal on his own at the hotel and an early night. After a few visits, he noticed that the people in the office were not as cooperative as they had been at the beginning. This puzzled him, and he asked one of his Dutch colleagues what had gone wrong. His colleague explained that they were no longer as motivated to work with him as they felt he had not taken the trouble to get to know them. Brian started to attend the Friday *borrelje* occasionally and relationships with his colleagues improved.

LEADERSHIP AND DECISION MAKING

A Dutch senior manager will have experience and expertise, as well as a good standard of education. Managers see themselves as "first among equals" and are encouraged to cultivate a straightforward style. It is expected that a decision will be reached only when all the parties concerned have conducted a full analysis. The manager takes responsibility for the success or failure of the project, and the final indicator of success will almost always be profitability, although the Dutch are very environmentally and socially aware and corporate social responsibility (CSR) issues will take priority over profit in some circumstances.

Dutch managers tend to avoid status symbols such as large expense accounts and a big car, as extravagance is frowned upon. As befits an egalitarian ethos, it is important for them to be prepared to listen to all levels of the company. Younger organizations tend to have a flatter matrix hierarchy, with far fewer levels, in order to encourage team work and to ease communication.

Taking advantage of one's superior position, making decisions unilaterally, intolerance, and attacking another's position without justification are all ways of losing employees' and colleagues' respect. A good Dutch manager will come across as confident, friendly, energetic, and ready to "get his or her hands dirty." Questions should be answered frankly and directly and should not be avoided. Willingness to debate and to listen to subordinates is prized, even though this inevitably slows down the decision making. Managers are expected to be well organized, to deal in facts, not sentiment, and to set clear objectives and targets.

MEETINGS AND NEGOTIATIONS

Dutch meetings are mainly for making decisions and clarifying procedures. There will usually be a clear timetable and an agenda, which will be adhered to.

Dress may be formal or informal but clean and smart. People may take off their jackets during a meeting (as in Britain, it is a sign of getting down to work)— follow the lead of the Dutch people present. Seating is normally informal and people sit where they are comfortable. Many virtual teams have meetings with their colleagues using telecom or Internet networks.

The pace of the meeting will be steady. The aims and objectives will have been clearly stated and the atmosphere will be reasonably serious. Technical issues will be presented in sufficient detail to enable full consideration, and participants will be expected to bring with them (and to have read) all the relevant documents. You will be expected be prepared to state your views on matters up for discussion—other people's time should be respected.

The Dutch are past masters at negotiation. Their aims are to get a favorable deal, with long-term profit, and to establish long-term relationships. They may put pressure on you to make decisions, and they will not be above bluffing about their own aims in order to find out your true objectives. They expect to debate plans with you in detail, and distrust intuition unsupported by facts. However, they are open to innovation, and if terms are clearly laid out they are willing to compromise.

CONTRACTS

Business matters—employment, the provision of goods or services, mergers and acquisitions, distribution, franchising agreements, and so on— are governed by Dutch civil law, which is based on a body of written codes and statues, the Dutch Civil Code (Burgerlijk Wetboek).

There is an accepted way of drawing up contracts and some aspects will be mandatory, that is, set by civil law. Others will be discretionary, and the parties involved can make a joint decision about them. Legal terminology cannot always be understood when translated from one language to another, and there is plenty of room for misunderstanding and misinterpretation, so to be on the safe side make the terms of the contract as specific as possible and get legal advice and support if you are at all unsure.

You can alter or withdraw terms during the negotiation stage but this has to be done within a reasonable amount of time, and you need to have been clear with the other party that you are still working out terms. Once you reach agreement, the contract is established and becomes legally binding.

Verbal agreements are also legally binding. However, in a commercial dispute in the Netherlands you need to show that you have a contract, so if you agree one verbally it is best to get it confirmed in writing and signed by all parties. The written contract supports (and provides evidence about) the verbal one, although the verbal one is still legally binding whether there is written confirmation or not. Be aware that there are some types of contract (for example, a purchase contract) that it is illegal to agree verbally. It is best to check with a lawyer if you are not sure if this rule applies to you.

HANDLING DISAGREEMENTS

The Dutch prefer to express disagreement honestly in a forthright manner and to resolve matters by logical argument. This means that you should be prepared for intense debate and to support everything you say with facts and data. Be as honest as you can, and respect others' right to disagree. It is important to speak up about disagreement. Silence may be seen as tacit acceptance. Avoid expressions such as "I can tell you in confidence" or "between you and me." This goes against the Dutch spirit of openness.

A key principle in Dutch law is the judgment of "fairness and reasonableness." This means that all parties in a dispute are required to have taken care of the other parties in the deal and to have treated them reasonably and fairly.

The Dutch are not a particularly litigious nation. They usually prefer to settle disputes amicably out of court, in order to save both time and money and to maintain good relationships. There is a Dutch National Arbitration Institute (Stichting Nederlands Arbitrage Instituut) that can provide registered qualified mediators to act as a neutral third party in disputes between employees and employers, or between different parties to a contract. The mediators are required in the Netherlands to follow procedural rules. Mediation is not legally binding, so if it fails to resolve matters the next step would be to go to arbitration. This is a process whereby the facts of the matter are considered by a judge (sometimes by up to three judges) and a ruling is then given, which is legally binding. This can entail the payment of damages and/or specific action to be taken by one or more of the parties concerned.

It is useful to note that where there is an uneven power balance, Dutch law will favor the weaker party— for example, the employee rather than the employer—so this needs to be taken into consideration by managers in a business context when dealing with staff disputes.

chapter nine

COMMUNICATING

LANGUAGE

Dutch is spoken in the Netherlands, and Flemish is spoken in parts of Belgium and the northwest of France. There is very little difference between the two—about the same as between American, British, and Australian English. Frisian, a minority Germanic language, is spoken in the northwestern province of Friesland.

Many Dutch people speak excellent English (it is the main foreign language taught in schools). It is often difficult to practice speaking Dutch, because so many people reply to you in English, but try at least to learn the basics, for occasions when it would be polite to use it, as this will be much appreciated. Do be aware that some people use English swear words when exclaiming, which they have picked up from English-language films and television programs. As they are a small country and a trading nation, the Dutch also have a working knowledge of other languages, such as German and French.

FAMILIAR AND POLITE FORMS OF ADDRESS

The Dutch have different words both for the singular and plural pronoun "you" and for the formal and informal "you." The informal you is "*je*" (plural "*jullie*"), and the formal is "*u*" (both singular and plural). When addressing older people, or if you are in a formal context, it is better to use the "*u*" form until you are invited to switch to "*je*." Err on the side of politeness rather than risk giving offense.

Up until fairly recently, "*je*" was used only for family and close friends but this has now changed and attitudes are far more relaxed. Generally speaking, you can use the "*je*" form to speak to people who are younger than you are, or around the same age. If you have already been invited to call someone by their first name, "*je*" is the correct form to use.

GREETINGS IN SHOPS

Up until a few years ago it was customary for people working in shops to address customers as "*u*." However, younger people are so used to addressing everybody as "*je*" that this has now become widespread and acceptable. You will usually be greeted in a shop with "*Goede morgen*," "*Goede middag*," or "*Goeden avond*," or good morning, afternoon, or evening. If you can cope with trying out the gutteral "*g*" sound, it is best to reply in kind. If not, then reply pleasantly in English. This prompts the sales personnel in many shops to switch to English to put you at ease.

When you have completed your purchase, the salesperson will say good-bye and may well wish you a good day. "*Dag*" (or "*tot ziens*") "*meneer/mevrouw en een prettige dag* (or *avond*) *verder*"—"Good-bye" (or "until the next time") "sir/madam and enjoy the rest of your day (or evening)." You can reply "*Dag*" or "*tot ziens*."

WRITTEN COMMUNICATIONS
Written Dutch is more formal than spoken, and business letters often include set phrases that are considered the polite way to express matters on paper. When the Dutch send e-mails these are much less formal than letters and generally short and to the point; no space is wasted on niceties. This is intended to be direct and to save time—after all time is money.

MISINTERPRETATIONS
The Dutch soften the tone of what they are saying with small words such as *toch* (yet, still, for all that, all the same), *even* (just), or *een beetje* (a little). Unfortunately, when they are speaking English these subtle modifications can be lost in translation and it can make them sound too direct and forceful. The Dutch are not shy about giving their opinion, but when speaking English they can sometimes sound as if they are insisting that you do things their way, rather than making a suggestion. This can lead native English-speakers to misinterpret what is being said to them and the manner in which it is being said, and to take offense when none has been intended.

HUMOR
Judging from the popularity of English-language sitcoms on Dutch and cable television, you would think that the Dutch sense of humor is very similar

to the American or British. In some respects it is. The Dutch like to poke fun at the establishment and they also appreciate humor that involves wordplay, repartee, and mimicry. Popular cabaret acts are often based upon this approach, with some bawdiness and slapstick thrown in for good measure.

In fact, much of the humor is based upon teasing and bringing people into line, reflecting the "*Doe maar gewoon . . .*" principle—letting people know their faults in a lighthearted way and ensuring that they do not take themselves too seriously. If you are on the receiving end of the teasing you are expected to take it in good part.

CONVERSATION

Very few topics of conversation are taboo. Perhaps the only one that is off-limits is how much people earn or the value of their possessions. The Dutch enjoy conversation over glasses of beer or countless cups of coffee. The livelier it gets, the better. You can expect people to give their opinions on all sorts of matters—sex, politics, religion, the weather, the royal family, education, whatever has been on television the night before, or in the newspapers. They also like to discuss what is going on in their local community.

They are usually keen to find out what you think as well. At times, it becomes so boisterous that it is difficult to make yourself heard. People are eager to get their own point of view across. To outsiders, this can seem very heated, but don't worry. Once the conversation has ended everybody arranges to meet again and goes home good friends.

Be prepared to join in both the social chat and the serious discussions. Take the lead from your Dutch friends. If they feel comfortable with you they will broaden the conversation to include more topics. It is unusual to discuss personal difficulties in a group—emotional issues are more commonly discussed on a one-to-one basis. Conversely, you may find that total strangers, perhaps on the train, will ask you some extremely direct questions about current issues. This is because you will be regarded as representative of your country, and they will want to hear what you have to say about your own country's affairs or how you view theirs. You can be frank, but be prepared to support what you say with a good argument.

BODY LANGUAGE

The Dutch are a straightforward lot; they look people in the eye and expect the same in return. If you don't do this, you may be regarded as rather shifty and untrustworthy. Dutch people are friendly, and will shake hands or give a light embrace when kissing cheeks in greeting (for members of the opposite sex), but otherwise they keep their distance physically. If you are the type of person who touches people as you are speaking to them, or gives them a bear hug when you arrive or leave, you may need to tone it down.

In a business setting it is rare for people to use personal space or their environment to intimidate staff or colleagues, or to demonstrate their status. Most managers have a desk and a table in their office. If somebody comes to talk to them, they will usually come out from behind their desk and sit with the person at the table, so that they are on a more equal footing. Even at board meetings, there is rarely a set place for the chairperson to sit, and people just sit where they are comfortable. Your body language should show that you are relaxed and confident, and should not be used to put other people at a disadvantage.

Body language in the Netherlands is generally very similar to that in Britain, although it is possibly more reserved than in some areas of America. Whatever else you do, make sure that your handshake is firm and that your smile reaches your eyes!

THE MEDIA
The Press

The Dutch media is wide-ranging and outspoken—within the bounds of laws against libel and discrimination. There is a large number of Dutch national and regional newspapers, and also a huge variety of magazines available. The key newspapers (all now produced in condensed format) are: *De Telegraaf* (equivalent to the British *Daily Mail* in style

and content),
*Het Financieele
Dagblad* (a
business and
finance paper
akin to the
Financial Times),
De Volkskrant (a
quality newspaper
on the political
left), *Algemeen
Dagblad* (a
politically neutral
broadsheet), and

the *NRC Handelsblad* (a business-orientated evening
paper). There are no Sunday papers, although there
are some weekend editions. Free papers are available
on the trains—the *Metro* and the *Spits*—and many
residential areas have free weeklies that are delivered
to your door.

It is possible to buy English-language newspapers
from main railway stations and at some newsdealers.
Several Dutch English-language publications cater
to expatriates and visiting business people. See
www.expatica.com/nl or www.dutchnews.nl for a
daily summary of the Dutch news.

TV and Radio
Dutch non-commercial TV is funded from central
government grants and topped up by a limited
amount of advertising. The Dutch Broadcasting
Association (De Nederlandse Omroep Stichting) is an
umbrella organization that coordinates broadcasting
on the national television and radio network. Public

broadcasting covers three television channels and five radio channels, plus a number of themed channels, all of which are required to reflect the diversity of Dutch society and to cater to different interests. There are also a number of commercial channels whose revenue comes through advertising.

Radio airtime is divided up in a similar manner. The original idea behind the system was to ensure that the population was exposed to a variety of ideas, as each broadcasting company had a different ideology. It is now increasingly difficult to detect any difference in the program content of the broadcasting companies. The Evangelische Omroep (EO) is regarded as an exception as it still promotes a definite religious message and specific values.

The Dutch cable-TV system enables the viewing public to choose between programs from several other countries, including Britain, France, Germany, Belgium, Italy, America, and Turkey. It is also possible to tune into radio stations from abroad.

TELEPHONE AND INTERNET

The vast majority of people in the Netherlands use cell phones and there are a large number of cell phone companies—their shops can be found on all main shopping streets. Be aware that non-EU citizens may be refused a contract by some providers. It is illegal to use a cell phone in a car unless you have a hands-free system.

The fixed-line telephone system is run primarily by KPN-Telecom, although it is now possible to use other companies and costs have been driven down. The country code for the Netherlands is 31 and each area of the country has its own local code.

You can dial anywhere directly from public telephones in the Netherlands. Within the country dial 0 and the area code; from overseas dial 00 31 and the area code without the 0. To dial out of the Netherlands, dial 00 before the country code number—for example 00 44 for Britain. For directory inquiries for numbers within the Netherlands, dial 0900 8008. For overseas directory inquiries, dial 0900 8418. You can use the local phone book for residential numbers, or the *Gouden Gids* (Yellow Pages) for business numbers.

Coin-operated public telephones have been phased out and replaced by card-operated phones. You can use your credit card to pay, but it is generally more convenient to buy a phone card. These can be obtained at post offices, newsstands, and railway stations. Some post offices also have public telephones.

When a Dutch person answers the telephone, they give their name, for example, "*Met Yvonne van der Gouw*," literally, "with Yvonne van der Gouw."

Generally speaking, it is not advisable to call people after 10:00 p.m. Even if they are not actually in bed, they are likely to be winding down and will not appreciate the disturbance.

There are lots of Internet service providers in the Netherlands offering one of two main forms of Internet access—cable or ADSL (Asynchronous Double Switched Line). Generally the connections are of high quality.

MAIL

Post offices (PTT) are open Monday to Friday from 8:30 a.m. to 5:00 p.m., and on Saturday from 8:30 a.m. to 12 noon or 1:00 p.m. Most of the staff in post offices speak good English and are happy to help and advise you. Stamps (*postzegels*) can also be purchased in many newsdealers, souvenir shops, and tobacconists. Mail boxes can be found on streets and outside post offices. Local mail goes into one slot and the rest into the other (*Overige Postcodes*, Other Postal Codes).

CONCLUSION

The Dutch are an admirable, complex people. Despite superficial similarities with modern American and British culture, they have a distinct take on the world, born of a proud tradition of self-reliance, fair dealing, and enterprise. In order to give a broad picture of Dutch society we have had to generalize—to explain what "normally" happens in particular situations. Of course, as with any society there are many subcultures. There are sections of society that adhere to very traditional Dutch values. There are also many groups who are happy to look outside the Netherlands for new ideas, especially in this age of globalization. The Internet and other communication networks have greatly accelerated this process.

Today, the character of Dutch society is under threat from the creation of a homogeneous international culture. Some members of Dutch society have reacted to this with wariness and are concerned that Dutch values and culture may be lost. The vast majority welcome people from other nationalities, although newcomers are now expected to make more of an effort to fit in with Dutch society—to learn the language and to find out about Dutch culture.

Dutch traditions of fairness and social justice are important to the world. Their business acumen and practical common sense benefit us all. A world without the Dutch sense of curiosity, zest for life, and unique balance of liberalism and conservatism would be a poorer place. The Netherlands offers the open-minded visitor a refreshing point of view, a lively cultural scene, and real pleasure to be found in the company of its friendly and engaging people.

Further Reading

Boucke, Laurie and Colin White. *The Undutchables—An Observation of the Netherlands: Its Culture and Inhabitants*. Colorado: White/Boucke Publishing, 2013.

Coates, Ben. *Why the Dutch are Different: A Journey into the Hidden Heart of the Netherlands*. London: Nicholas Brealey Publishing, 2017.

De Rooi, Maarten (author), Jurjen Drenth (illustrator). *New Visions of the Netherlands* (English version). Alphen aan de Rijn: Dutch Publishers, 2013.

Fuller, Mark (ed.). *Alphabet Soup—Decoding Terms in Dutch Business, Politics and Society*. Amsterdam/Antwerp: Business Contact/Het Financieel Dagblad, 2001.

Gazaleh-Weevers, Sheila, and Connie Moser and Shirley Agndo. *Here's Holland*. Delft: Eburon Academic Publishers, 2007.

Schama, Simon. *The Embarrassment of Riches: An Interpretation of Dutch Culture in the Golden Age*. London: Vintage, 1997.

Van der Horst, Han. *The Low Sky—Understanding the Dutch*. Schiedam: Scriptum, 2015.

Vossestein, Jacob. *Dealing with the Dutch: The Cultural Context of Business and Work in the Netherlands*. Amsterdam: Kit Publishers, 2015.

The American Women's Club of The Hague. *At Home In Holland: A Practical Guide for Living in the Netherlands*. Delft: Eburon Academic Publishers, 2009.

Dijkstra, Stephanie. *The Holland Handbook: Your Guide to Living in the Netherlands*. Schiedam: Scriptum, 2017.

Van Marle, Jeroen. *The Rough Guide to the Netherlands*. London: Rough Guides, March 2016.

Le Nevez, Catherine. *Lonely Planet - The Netherlands (Travel Guide)*. London: Lonely Planet, 2016.

Le Nevez, Catherine, and Karla Zimmerman. *Lonely Planet Amsterdam (Travel Guide)*. London: Lonely Planet, 2016.

Useful General Web sites

www.expatica.com/nl
www.iamexpat.nl
www.expatfocus.com
www.angloinfo.com
www.access-nl.org
www.holland.com
www.nlplanet.com
www.iamsterdam.com

www.netherlands-tourism.com
www.dutchnews.nl
www.nltimes.nl
www.government.nl
www.cbs.nl/en
www.studyinholland.nl

Index